Warships of
the World:
Major Classes

No. CLO3 *Prat* (Light Cruiser) of the Chilean Navy.

Warships of
The World:
Major Classes

BERNARD IRELAND

LONDON

IAN ALLAN LTD

First published 1976
Reprinted 1978

ISBN 0 7110 0687 3

Published by Ian Allan Ltd, Shepperton, Surrey,
and printed in the United Kingdom by
The Garden City Press Limited, Letchworth,
Hertfordshire, SG6 1JS

No. CGN 9 *Long Beach* Guided Missile Cruiser
(see page 65).

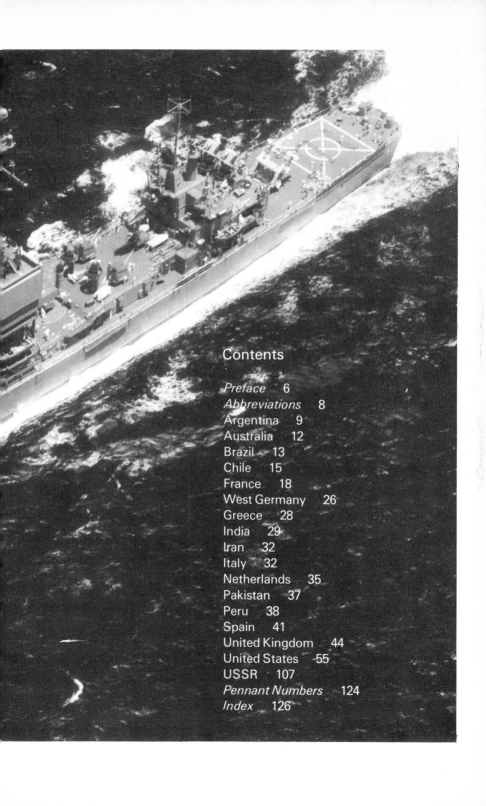

Contents

Preface

This volume is planned to be the first of three, the others being Escort Ships and Submarines/Minor Warships. The approach is made with a broad brush and seeks to offer a comparison between equivalent contemporary classes of warship in the world's navies, giving, where space allows, some background detail.

The term 'Major Warship Classes' is not definitive and the author has, therefore, dealt with surface warships with a standard tonnage exceeding 5,000. Such an arbitrary definition inevitably leads to anomalies and, should the reader feel strongly about the inclusion or non-inclusion of specific classes, his indulgence is requested pending the appearance of the second volume.

The large warship, by virtue of cost and complexity, is becoming increasingly the prerogative of the two major naval powers and a book on the subject is, necessarily, devoted in great part to two fleets. Warship development is composed largely of one power's efforts to neutralise an advance on the part of another and warship designs of the last twenty years have been dominated by one of two major developments, viz. the guided missile and the nuclear submarine. These have dictated weaponry and electronics which have, in turn, defined the ship—which is, after all, only the package which delivers them.

Those simpler warships that still survive are most under the flags of the smaller navies and are no normally of advancing years. They are ou numbered by the greater mass of units of the la two decades which have grown ever mo complicated. Electronics, however, advance rapid and many of these complexities are outdated often before the entry of the ship into servic Thus, a case could be made for a return to th 'pure' design where a simple unit has recognise limitations which are offset by its cheapness an which will require the co-operation of a mo refined escort for certain missions. Certain design such as the British Type 14 frigate and the ne American Sea Control Ship go some way in th proposed direction; others, such as the great number of Russian escorts and the America LHA's, have an omni-purpose design and continu a trend which will be directed in the final analysis b financial considerations.

Within the limited compass of each ship descri tion, jargon has been avoided but there mu inevitably be a certain number of technical terms

s with any major subject. Certain of these are
referred to in abbreviated fashion and a list of these
terms is included.

Russian ships and their equipment have recognised
NATO code names and these are normally used.
These names are not carried by individual ships,
e.g. the *Kuril* class consists of *Kiev* and *Minsk;*
there is no *Kuril.*

Dimensions of larger vessels are usually quoted to
the nearest foot and displacement to the nearest
one hundred tons. Not only are these parameters
then easier to remember but are probably more
realistic — after all, a large ship can expand or
contract a foot quite easily with temperature
variation and can consume a hundred tons of fuel in
a day's hard steaming!

Ships are grouped simply under their respective
flags, which are placed in alphabetical order. This
system has disadvantages when compared with
grouping under types, which can then be
compared directly. This latter method was not
used, however, due to the rather confusing
number of official terms for what are basically the
same types of ship.

Acknowledgement must be given to the many
sources of illustration which were tapped, with
special mention to the US Naval Information
Service, whose task was of considerable
magnitude.

The active job of obtaining this mass of pictures
was cheerfully undertaken by Penny Grant, in
whose debt I am.

Lastly, my wife, whose unenviable position it was
to type this mountain of information, sorting out
my tangled grammar simultaneously with decipher-
ing the handwriting in which it was written.

Bernard Ireland
Fareham, 1975

Kresta II class (Guided Missile Cruiser) of the Soviet
Navy.

Abbreviations

AA (W)	Anti-aircraft (Warfare)	**LSD**	Landing Ship, Dock
AC	Aircraft	**LSM**	Landing Ship, Mechanised
ACS	Aircraft Carrier Squadron	**LST**	Landing Ship, Tank
AEW	Airborne Early Warning	**LSV**	Landing Ship, Vehicle
AGC	Amphibious Force Flagships	**LVT**	Amphibious Tractors
AGF	Miscellaneous Command Ship	**MCS**	Mine Countermeasures Ship
AKA	Attack Cargo Ship	**mm**	Millimetre
AN	Net Layer	**MSL**	Minesweeping Launch
AP	Transport	**NTDS**	Naval Tactical Data System
APA	Attack Transport	**q.v.**	Quod Vide (which see)
ASROC	Anti-submarine Rocket	**RAN**	Royal Australian Navy
AS (W)	Anti-submarine (Warfare)	**RIM**	Shipborne Anti-aircraft Missile
AVT	Auxiliary Aircraft Transport	**RNN**	Royal Netherlands Navy
BB	Battleship	**SAM**	Surface-to-air Missile
BPDMS	Basic Point Defence Missile System	**SCS**	Sea Control Ship
CA	Heavy Cruiser	**shp**	Shaft Horse Power
CAG	Guided Missile Heavy Cruiser	**SSM**	Surface-to-surface Missile
CC	Command Ship	**TT**	Torpedo Tube
CCA	Carrier-Controlled Approach	**VDS**	Variable-depth Sonar
CG	Guided Missile Cruiser	**V/STOL**	Vertical/Short Take-off and Land
CGN	Nuclear Propelled Guided Missile Cruiser	**WW I**	World War I
CIWS	Close-in Weapons System	**WW II**	World War II
CL	Light Cruiser	**3-D**	Three-dimensional
CLG	Guided Missile Light Cruiser		
CLGN	Nuclear-propelled Guided Missile Light Cruiser		
CM	Minelaying Cruiser		
CODAG	Combined Diesel and Gas (Turbines)		
COSAG	Combined Steam and Gas (Turbines)		
CV	Aircraft Carrier		
CVA	Attack Aircraft Carrier		
CVAN	Nuclear-propelled Attack Aircraft Carrier		
CVB	Large Aircraft Carrier		
CVL	Light Aircraft Carrier		
CVS	Anti-submarine Aircraft Carrier		
CVT	Training Aircraft Carrier		
DLG	Guided Missile Frigate		
DLGN	Nuclear-propelled Guided Missile Frigate		
DP	Dual Purpose		
ECM	Electronic Countermeasures		
FPB	Fast Patrol Boat		
FRAM	Fleet Rehabilitation and Modernisation		
GRP	Glass reinforced plastic		
HA	High Angle		
HNMS	Her Netherlands Majesty's Ship		
In.	Inch		
LAMPS	Light Airborne Multi-purpose System		
LCA	Landing Craft, Assault		
LCC	Amphibious Command Ship		
LCM	Landing Craft, Mechanised		
LCT	Landing Craft, Tank		
LCU	Landing Craft, Utility		
LCVP	Landing Craft, Vehicle and Personnel		
LHA	General-purpose Amphibious Assault Ship		
LKA	Amphibious Cargo Ship		
LOA	Length overall		
LPA	Amphibious Transport		
LPD	Amphibious Transport Dock		
LPH	Amphibious Assault Ship		

25 de Mayo Aircraft Carrier   Argentina

Units: *25 de Mayo* (ex-HNMS *Karel Doorman,* ex-
HMS *Venerable*)
Laid Down: 1942
Completed: 1943
Launched: 1945
Displacement: 15,900 standard
19,900 Deep Load
Length (o.a.): 693ft
Beam: 80ft (121 over flight deck)
Draught: 25ft
Machinery: Geared turbines 2 shafts
40,000shp for 24 knots
Armament: 10 +40mm Bofors (10 × 1)
Aircraft: Max: 21 dependent upon size. Normal:
Eight fixed wing a/c.
Six helicopters
For others of same class, see:
Melbourne (Australia)
Minas Gerais (Brazil)
Vikrant (India)

The Royal Navy rapidly discovered the necessity
for fleet air support from the earliest days of World
War II. Fleet carriers could not be laid down in any
large numbers as their complexity would obviously
preclude completion during the estimated period of
hostilities. Sterling service was rendered by the
'Woolworth' utility carriers but these were not large
enough for fleet work. Two intermediate classes,
known as Light Fleet Carriers, were therefore laid
down in British yards. There was the *Colossus* class
of ten ships and the *Majestic* class of six.

To save design time, the hull lines were basically
mercantile, were built merchant ship fashion and
under Lloyds survey.

Even these corner cuttings were not sufficient,

however, to get more than a handful complete by
the end of the war. Four of the *Colossus* class
managed to arrive in the Far East to form the 11th
ACS before close of hostilities. They saw little
action, but *Colossus* was detached as part of a
Task Group to re-occupy the Shanghai area after
the Japanese surrender.

With far too many ships to discharge its
peacetime duties, the Royal Navy embarked on a
massive scrap and transfer programme. Many
smaller navies benefited from the acquisition of
surplus ships, the Netherlands taking *Venerable* as
its first-ever aircraft carrier. She was transferred in
1948, hoisting the Dutch flag as the *Karel Doorman*
named after the commander of the Allied force
defeated at the Java Sea action of 1942. Where the
class had proved too small and slow for modern
Royal Navy operations, they were still too valuable
to be used as, say, convoy escorts. They were,
however, ideal for a smaller fleet with limited
resources.

Karel Doorman served with the RNN for seven
years until she had fallen well behind current
standards. From 1955 to 1958, therefore, she was
extensively modernised at a Rotterdam yard,
emerging with an angled deck, strengthened for
more modern and heavier aircraft such as
Seahawks and Avengers, steam catapult and
improved landing aids. Externally, the island had
been rebuilt with a towering mast and cowled
funnel which gave her an appearance unlike any of
her sisters. This dominating structure was crowned
by large Philips search and navigation antennae
with a curved height-finding array at either end of
the island (that at the after end was soon
removed).

There are two echeloned machinery spaces, each housing two boilers and an associated turbine set.

In 1965, the ageing boilers were replaced by those from the never-completed *Majestic*-class *Leviathan*. In 1968, there was a serious boiler-room fire and the ship was too badly damaged to be repaired economically for the Dutch fleet.

She escaped the breakers by being purchased by Argentina and was refitted, gaining the *Leviathan*'s turbines in the process.

Joining her new navy in 1969, she was renamed *25 de Mayo* (in full, *Vingesima Quinto de Mayo*), operating alongside her near-sister *Independencia* (ex-HMS *Warrior*). The latter ship was discarded in 1971, leaving the *25 de Mayo* as the sole aerial support afloat with the Argentine Navy.

She deploys A-4F Skyhawks and G-89 Trackers together with helicopters if necessary.

General Belgrano Cruiser   Argentina

Units: *General Belgrano* (ex-*17 de Octubre*, ex-*Phoenix*, CL46)
Nueve de Julio (ex-*Boise*, CL47)

	General Belgrano	Nueve de Julio
Laid Down:	1935	1935
Launched:	1938	1936
Completed:	1939	1939

Displacement: 10,700 standard average
13,700 Deep Load
Length (o.a.): 608ft
Beam: 69ft
Draught: 24ft
Machinery: Geared steam turbines 4 shafts
10,000shp for 32 knots
Armament: Fifteen—6-inch (5 × 3)
Eight—5-inch (8 × 1)
Twenty-eight—40mm (6 × 4) & (2 × 2)
Two helicopters

For others of same class, see:
Tamandare (Brazil)
Prat/O'Higgins (Chile)

At the close of World War II, the US Navy, like the RN, found itself with many warships superfluous to peacetime requirements. Scrapping was not quite as ruthless as on the British scale and much modern tonnage found its way to smaller, friendly navies. Some of those to benefit were the larger South American fleets, among them the Argentinian.

Its major warships were badly overage with the two battleships *Moreno* and *Rivadavia* dating from the great period of rivalry with Brazil before World War I and the coast defence ship *Pueyrredon* built before the turn of the century.

Contemporary naval thinking had made them redundant but a large gap would have been left in the naval ranks by scrapping without replacement.

The Argentine has a long coastline ranging well over 1,000 miles from the densely populated area around the Plate estuary to the inhospitable fastnesses of Tierra del Fuego. (In addition there is the disputed claim on the Falkland Islands.) The area needs ships of good range and seakeeping qualities to patrol it; in short, cruisers.

There were but three, the most powerful being the pair of *Almirante Browns*. Handsome, Italian-

General Belgrano

built ships, they proved a great disappointment in service so when an American offer of a couple of *Brooklyn*-class cruisers were made in 1951, it was welcome. It was part of a programme by the US to sell warships at a very low price, buttressing the strength of minor fleets whilst carefully avoiding a concentration of power in any one of them.

The ships transferred were the USS *Boise* and *Phoenix* which dated from 1939 and had seen an active war.

The dominant feature of the class is the heavy main battery of fifteen 6-inch guns in five triple turrets. Three of these are forward with 'B' turret superfiring over 'A' and 'C'. The latter turret normally faces aft, giving a silhouette reminiscent of Japanese heavy cruisers.

Eight 5-inch guns in open single mountings are disposed in the waist. A total of nearly forty smaller automatic weapons are carried, a legacy of the air war in the Pacific. *Gen Belgrano* (only) has had a pair of quadruple *Sea Cat* short range SAM's fitted in an effort at updating. Recently, the American search and gunnery radars have been removed to the favour of Dutch equipment, with which the Argentinians had become familiar on the *25 de Mayo*.

The typical higher American freeboard continues right aft to give a wide, high quarterdeck. Below this is a hangar spacious enough to house four aircraft which were operated by the large crane on the counter and two catapults, since removed. Two helicopters now occupy these quarters.

Belgrano on transfer was originally named *17 de Octubre*. This name had political connections with General Peron and the ship was renamed when he left office.

Ships of this type are primitive by today's standards and in view of their age and large complements, it cannot be long before they make way for smaller and more economical craft.

La Argentina Cruiser

Argentina

Units: No. C3 *La Argentina*
Laid Down: 1936
Launched: 1937
Completed: 1939
Displacement: 6,000 standard
8,600 Deep Load
Length (o.a.): 541ft
Beam: 57ft
Draught: 17ft
Machinery: Geared steam turbines 4 shafts
54,000shp for 30 knots (designed)
Armament: Nine—6-inch (3 × 3)
Fourteen—40mm (6 × 2) and (2 × 1)
Six—21-inch TT

This is a 'one-off' ship, designed to fulfil the functions of a cruiser whilst offering accommodation for over 130 cadets, who are able to work the ship and gain practical experience along with the theory. Few other purpose-built ships of this sort are met with but *Jeanne d'Arc* and *Deutschland* are used similarly under the French and German flags respectively.

Knuckled bows and 'Admiralty' funnels betray her British origins. She was completed by Vickers Armstrongs at Barrow in 1939 at a time when Britain was the major supplier of warships to the order of the Argentinians.

Her appearance is a blend of contemporary

British cruiser classes; in size and profile she is strongly reminiscent of the *Arethusas* of 1934 with the addition of a more powerful main battery, with triple 6-inch turrets which were being introduced into the *Southamptons* in 1936.

By accepting a modest penalty of two knots in speed some 10,000shp less were required when compared with the *Arethusas.* The smaller engines offset the extra weight of the armament and allow for the long forecastle deck to be built out to the sides over its full length back to the mainmast, providing the extra accommodation space for the cadets.

In the space between the after funnel and the mainmast were originally four 4-inch HA guns in open mountings. These were landed, however, in 1950, being replaced by twin 40mm weapons, others being added at the same time around the bridge.

The widely-spaced funnels are, of course, a function of the boiler room layout but originally left a conveniently open deck space for a catapult and a pair of Seagull amphibians. In accordance with post-war practice, both aircraft and gear have been landed. The crane has been retained, however, to handle the multitude of boats essential to training and which are now stowed in this area.

Below this deck, one level down, are sided triple torpedo tube mountings. Unlike normal British practice, these mountings are concealed by hinged covers which normally enclose them at sea.

Although the battleships have disappeared, the personnel strength of the Argentinian fleet has increased threefold since 1945. It would appear that *La Argentina* would be assured of a future except that she has now discharged over 35 years of service, a good span by warship standards. Her performance has inevitably deteriorated and, in view of the fact that two new British-designed Type 42 frigates are due to join the Argentinian fleet in 1975/6, she has been stricken from the active list after modernisation plans were abandoned. It is worth noting in this age of expensive manpower that *La Argentina's* normal complement of about 600 is sufficient to man both of the highly automated 42's.

Melbourne Aircraft Carrier

Australia

Units: *Melbourne* (ex-*Majestic*)
Laid Down: 1943
Launched: 1945
Completed: 1955
Displacement: 16,000 standard
20,000 Deep Load
Length (o.a.): 702ft
Beam: 80ft
Draught: 25ft
Machinery: Geared steam turbines 2 shafts
42,000shp for 24.5 knots
Armament: Twelve—40mm (4 × 2) + (4 × 1)
Aircraft: Dependent upon mix

For others of same class, see:
25 de Mayo (Argentina)
Minas Gerais (Brazil)
Vikrant (India)

The *Majestic* class of light fleet carrier was a group of six laid down at the end of 1943, about a year after the *Colossus* group. Although many short cuts were taken with design and construction and complexities kept to a minimum none was complete by the end of the war although all hulls had either been launched or carried to too advanced a stage of construction to be broken up

before a decision was taken regarding the likely roles and composition of the peacetime Royal Navy. The incomplete hulls were either laid up or brought to a launching state to clear valuable slips. Work was then stopped.

Thus it was that the *Majestic* class became noteworthy in that it saw practically no service under the White Ensign, its ships being completed to be transferred out of a shrinking RN.

The Commonwealth navies which had fought with such dedication alongside the RN had commenced at the outset of hostilities with squadrons of modest size, but had rapidly expanded with acquisition of responsibilities and battle experience. They had proved their right to greater postwar spheres of interest and the addition of air power to the major fleets was necessary if they were adequately to cover the vast areas of sea adjacent to them.

Two of the *Majestics* were allocated to the RAN. The first, HMS *Terrible,* was renamed *Sydney,* completed rapidly and arrived in Australia in 1949 in time to demonstrate the usefulness of the smaller carrier as she deployed Sea Fury and Firefly aircraft in the Korean War.

The second carrier was the class name ship, *Majestic,* which was renamed *Melbourne.* Having

lain idle since 1945, the hull was again taken in hand in 1949. Completion was a protracted process, however, as this was a time of great development in aircraft carrier design, a factor reflected in the design changes which delayed her eventual commissioning until 1955. She was a great improvement on her sister with an angled flight deck, strengthened for the operation of heavier jet aircraft such as the Sea Venom, a steam catapult and better landing aids.

On her delivery the older *Sydney* was relegated to a training role, serving as a fast transport to Vietnam before her disposal in 1973.

Melbourne underwent a further updating refit in 1969 when she was again strengthened and equipped to operate more modern and heavier types of aircraft.

Her strike power is now vested in the eight A-4G MDD Skyhawks that she carries with AS backup provided by half a dozen S-2E Grumman Trackers and Wessex helicopters. The latter have also a utility value.

Her appearance has changed little except in the addition of a lattice mast with TACAN and ECM pods, the large Philips-type search antenna atop the bridge and the American style CCA radar under the dome abaft the funnel.

Minas Gerais Aircraft Carrier   Brazil

Units: No. A11 *Minas Gerais* (ex-HMS *Vengeance*)
Laid Down: 1942
Launched: 1944
Completed: 1945
Displacement: 15,900 standard
19,900 Deep Load
Length (o.a.): 695ft
Beam: 80ft
Draught: 24ft
Machinery: Geared steam turbines 2 shafts 40,000shp for 24 knots
Armament: Ten—40mm (2 × 4) + (1 × 2)
Aircraft: About 20 dependent upon mix
For others of same class, see:
25 de Mayo (Argentina)
Melbourne (Australia)
Vikrant (India)

In spite of the rivalry that still exists between the larger South American fleets, it is comment on the complications and expense of maintaining a fleet air arm that, when Brazil acquired the ex-British *Vengeance* in 1956, no other neighbouring navy could follow suit for over a decade.

One of the ten-strong *Colossus* class, *Vengeance* was completed early in 1945 and arrived in the Far East in time only to witness the end of the Japanese war. Unlike the incomplete units of the light fleet carrier classes, she was not laid up but remained active in the RN, being modified among other duties for service in Arctic conditions.

The Australians, meanwhile, had commissioned a near sister into the RAN and requested a second. It was decided that this second unit, *Melbourne,*

was to have an extended modernising exercise on what was still an incomplete hull.

This involved strengthening and building-in an angled deck and steam catapult. Design changes made this a protracted business, eventually lasting some six years, from 1949 to 1955.

As an interim measure to help the RAN, HMS *Vengeance* was detached for service with them for the period 1953-5. She was returned on the eventual completion of *Melbourne,* her now experienced crew transferring to the new ship for the delivery voyage.

Like many ships who had spent a considerable spell under another flag, *Vengeance* came up for sale and her disposal to the Brazilians was announced in 1956.

She was renamed after the province of *Minas Gerais,* a name borne previously by one of a pair of Armstrong-built dreadnoughts that gave long service to the Brazilians. Like her sister *Venerable* (bought by the Dutch) she was sent to a Dutch yard for rebuilding to more modern standards. Different shipyards were involved and it is interesting to compare the different profiles of the rebuilt ships. The imposing funnel and complex arrays demanded by the larger navy were here unnecessary and the new superstructure was surmounted by a low, pot-like funnel and a simply equipped lattice mast. A clear angled deck and a steam catapult firing over the port bow were built in, together with improved landing aids and replacement elevators for larger and heavier aircraft. The conspicuous handling crane abaft the superstructure was removed.

She sailed for Brazil in 1961 with the capacity to

operate aircraft of up to about 9 tons in weight. The balance in carrier operations has, since then, swung more towards AS operations and a unit of this size is about ideal. Maintenance facilities were modified to enable the ship to operate Grumman S-2A Trackers for surveillance, detection and attack with backup supplied by Sikorsky SH-3D

Sea King Helicopters. As the ship does not have hull sonar equipment, the aircraft must rely on sonobuoys for tracking.

Properly integrated with her escort, this unsophisticated ship can still pose a real threat to an enemy submarine.

Tamandare Light Cruiser Brazil

Units: *Tamandare* No. C12 (ex-*St. Louis* CL49)
Laid Down: 1936
Launched: 1938
Completed: 1939
Displacement: 10,000 standard
13,400 Deep Load
Length: 608ft
Beam: 69ft
Draught: 24ft
Machinery: Geared steam turbines 4 shafts
100,000shp for 32 knots
Armament: Fifteen—6-inch (5 × 3)
Eight—5-inch (T-(4 × 2); B-(8 × 1) !
Twenty-eight—40mm
One helicopter
For others of same class, see:

Belgrano }
9 de Julio } Argentina

O'Higgins }
Prat } Chile

At the end of World War II, the US Navy found itself with large numbers of surplus ships. These were disposed of by scrapping, placing in low level reserve, by transfer or by sale at giveaway prices to friendly navies.

Beneficiaries in the last category were the 'ABC' navies of South America which were allowed to purchase a pair of large light cruisers apiece. This

was a nice solution from the US Government's point of view; it buttressed the strength of these fleets with reasonably modern ships without giving advantage to any one of them, the US being well aware of the traditional rivalries existing.

Whereas the Argentinian and Chilean Navies bought two *Brooklyn* class apiece, the Brazilians came by one of this type and one of the closely similar *St. Louis* class. The name ship of the latter class was transferred early in 1951 and renamed *Tamandare* after an early C-in-C of the Brazilian fleet. The *St. Louis* were really a modified Brooklyn rather than a separate class, being contemporary in construction although completed about a year later.

Hulls were of about the same dimensions and the same unusual main battery disposition was retained. This was in five triple 6-inch turrets, three forward and two aft. 'B' turret was elevated to superfire over 'A' and 'C' which were mounted at the same level with the latter's gun barrels pointing aft when housed.

The major external difference was in the superstructure layout. The *Brooklyns* had a basic open layout close akin to other pre-war classes such as the *New Orleans* or *Wichita,* but the new sub-class lost the large distinctive gap between the after funnel and after superstructure around the mainmast. The after directors were thus sited much

further forward and the automatic AA armament commanded better firing arcs around the more compact midships structure. This close grouping of funnels and masts was retained through a succession of American war-built cruiser classes.

A further improvement was the regrouping of the eight secondary 5-inch guns. These had been in open, single mountings which looked rather vulnerable. In their place were shipped four twin gunhouses, quite large and placed surprisingly high up.

Similar aircraft arrangements were provided. Catapults have since been landed but the crane and hangar have been retained, giving a useful helicopter capacity.

As early as 1948 it was announced that the *St. Louis* was to be acquired by the Peruvian navy,

then without major units, but the sale fell through with the Peruvians waiting another decade before finally purchasing cruisers from the UK.

The second cruiser purchased by Brazil was the *Brooklyn* class *Philadelphia*, renamed *Barroso*. She was, however, discarded in 1973 and dismantled in 1974. In light of war experience, this class was retro-fitted with bulges and the superstructure reduced, suggesting that action damage could easily prejudice stability.

Brazil is now acquiring six British-designed guided missile destroyers of the Thornycroft Mark 10 type. With their smaller crews and greater punch they will probably render the conventional *Tamandare* redundant and the time of her disposal cannot be far away.

Latorre Light Cruiser

Units: *Almirante Latorre* (ex-*Gota Lejon*)
Laid Down: 1943
Launched: 1945
Completed: 1947
Displacement: 8,200 standard
9,200 Deep Load
Length (o.a.): 597ft
Beam: 54ft
Draught: 22ft
Machinery: Geared steam turbines 2 shafts
100,000shp for 33 knots
Armament: Seven—6-inch (1 × 3) + (2 × 2)
Four—57mm (4 × 1)
Eleven—40mm
Six—21-inch TT (2 × 3)
120 mines

Note. *Sister* Tre Kronor *discarded by Swedish Navy in 1964*

Chile

Sweden, a country with a long history of neutrality nevertheless maintains a small but well-balanced fleet. Operations geared to national defence are centred around the shallow, skerry-ridden waters of the Baltic and its approaches. All distances involved are small and the threat from hostile aircraft would be ever-present. These operating limitations have resulted in the evolution of highly individual designs, most of them capable of more than one function.

At the outbreak of World War II, the backbone of the fleet lay in a handful of antiquated, armoured coast defence ships, slow and with poor AA defence. These were to be rather tardily reinforced by a pair of cruisers but, after much re-casting of designs, these were not laid down until 1943 and finished in 1947 long after the cessation of hostilities.

Named *Gota Lejon* (Gothic Lion) and *Tre Kronor*

15

(Three Crowns, the national emblem), their rakish appearance resembled no other class in any fleet. A long forecastle deck with little sheer ran aft as far as X-turret, the long, low quarterdeck terminating in a fine-lined spoon stern of rather Germanic aspect; the whole gave an impression of weatherliness and speed.

The German allusion could be taken also to main armament disposition. To save top-weight, a superimposed 'B' turret was not fitted, partial compensation for its loss being made by making the lone forward turret a triple. The break of the forecastle deck allowed a normal layout for two turrets in 'X' and 'Y' positions. This 'one forward, two aft' layout was common in both cruisers and destroyers of the German fleet of World War II.

Wisely not attempting too much on a limited displacement the designers made the after turrets twins, giving an unusual main battery of seven 150mm weapons. They are of high (70°) elevation and can operate in an AA role.

A rather low, 'bitty' superstructure was set off by two funnels with very heavy rakes and the two tripod masts carried gunnery radar from the outset.

Stability may still have been a problem on the light draught for, only four years after completion, the ships were reconstructed. Alterations included

a new, compact bridge structure which brought the main director down one level.

As with most shallow-water navies, minelaying capacity is important. This class was equipped with rails running the length of the quarterdeck on either side, emerging from apertures on either side of 'X' barbette. Triple torpedo tubes are still sided at this point.

A further modernisation in 1958 improved AA armament and new radars of Dutch and British manufacture were fitted.

The large conventionally-armed warship became particularly vulnerable in confined waters on the advent of the guided missile and the Swedes discarded the *Tre Kronor* in 1964. *Gota Lejon* was kept on until 1971 when her sale to Chile was announced.

Chile's immense coastline, spanning about 40° of latitude from the sub-tropics to the Horn needs weatherly ships of good endurance for its policing and the cruiser still has a real part to play.

The earlier ship bearing the name *Latorre* was a battleship building in the UK at the outbreak of WW I. She was appropriated by the British Government, serving as HMS *Canada,* and seeing action at Jutland before her eventual handover to Chile after the Armistice. She lasted until 1958.

Prat Light Cruiser   Chile

Units: No. CLO2 *O'Higgins* (ex-*Brooklyn* CL40)
No. CLO3 *Prat* (ex-*Nashville* CL43)

	O'Higgins	Prat
Laid Down:	1935	1935
Launched:	1936	1937
Completed:	1938	1938
Displacement:		
Standard	9,700	10,000
Deep Load	13,000	13,500

Length (o.a.): 608ft
Beam: 69ft
Draught: 24ft
Machinery: Geared steam turbines 4 shafts 100,000shp for 32 knots
Armament: Fifteen—6-inch (5 × 3)
Eight—5-inch (8 × 1)
Twenty-eight—40mm
One helicopter

No. CL03 *Prat*

For others of same class, see:
Belgrano
Nueve de Julio } Argentina
Tamandare   Brazil

The post-war US reinforcement of South American navies involved the transfer, in addition to various flotilla vessels, of six large light cruisers of the *Brooklyn* and *St. Louis* classes. Two each went to the major navies of Argentina, Brazil and Chile at a low fraction of their true value. The Chilean pair were *Brooklyn* herself and her sister *Nashville.*

As a class, the *Brooklyns* were only some seven years old at the end of World War II but the war had advanced the technology of warships to such a degree that they were outdated. The refits and modernisation that they required were not justified because they were superfluous to peacetime naval requirements. They were therefore among the first to be decommissioned.

The cruisers that were transferred well fitted the requirements of countries with long, exposed coastlines with few support bases. A range of 15,000 miles at 15 knots was backed by a useful — and imposing — main battery of no less than fifteen 6-inch guns in five triple turrets. Radar and machinery fits were simple but adequate, and what is important, did not overload the limited technical backup that could be afforded.

Some confusion prefaced the allocation of individual ships. In 1949, the *Boise* was named for transfer to Chile, but she eventually went to Argentina.

In addition to the nine 6-inch forward and six aft, there are eight 5-inch weapons, disposed in single open mountings in the waist, their crews rather vulnerable to splinters or strafing aircraft.

Experience against mass aircraft strikes in the Pacific War had led the Americans to fit large numbers of 40mm and 20mm weapons wherever

suitable sites could be found. Thus this class had 28 and 24 of these respectively and a large proportion of these are still fitted.

The high quarterdeck overlies the aircraft space. Originally up to four floatplanes could be accommodated comfortably. These are gone, together with their two catapults, although the handling crane has been retained and the hangar now houses a pair of helicopters.

The class is quite well protected with up to four inches of armour on the hull and five on turret roofs. Bulges were added after they were completed to improve stability following severe action damage.

With Argentina and Brazil acquiring new tonnage with powerful missile armaments their cruisers will soon be redundant.

Chile's choice, however, has been a pair of British-built Leanders. These normally deploy only the short range Seacat SAM, but the Chilean pair have been fitted with four Exocet SSM launchers in place of the VDS. It will be interesting to see if they are regarded as replacements for the ageing conventionally-armed cruisers or whether these will have to soldier on for a while.

The name *O'Higgins* is a reminder of the large number of Europeans — particularly Irishmen — who distinguished themselves in the independence wars in several South American states.

17

Clemenceau Aircraft Carrier   France

Units: No. PA54/R98 *Clemenceau*
No. PA55/R99 *Foch*

	Clemenceau	*Foch*
Laid Down:	1955	1957
Launched:	1957	1960
Completed:	1961	1963

Displacement: 27,300 standard
32,800 Deep Load
Length (o.a.): 869ft
Beam: 104ft
Draught: 24.5ft
Width: 168ft (over flight deck)
Machinery: Geared steam turbines 2 shafts
126,000shp for 32 knots
Armament: Eight—3.9-inch (100mm) (8 × 1)

The French, like other major navies, founded a naval air arm with the aid of converted tonnage but various circumstances militated against construction of home-designed carriers until quite late.

Under the scrap-or-convert clause of the Washington Treaty, the incomplete battleship *Béarn* was rebuilt into a 22,000-ton carrier. In 1938, the first purpose-built carrier, *Joffre*, was laid down but was overtaken by World War II and scrapped on the stocks.

Béarn served with the Free French Navy during World War II but only as an aircraft transport due to her low speed. For this reason the escort carrier *Biter* was transferred in 1945 from the RN, being renamed *Dixmude* and then supplemented in 1946 by the ex-Colossus class carrier *Arromanches*. Both of these have since been discarded.

1947 saw authorisation given for the construction of a 16,000-ton carrier to be named *Clemenceau*, but the project was delayed and the gap filled by the loan of two escort carriers, *La Fayette* and *Bois Belleau* from the US Navy.

The *Clemenceau* project was again given the green light in 1953, followed in 1955 by authorisation for a sister ship, *Foch*. Each took six years to build, emerging in 1961 and 1963 at nearly twice the tonnage of the original 1947 project.

In profile, they are strongly reminiscent of the American *Essex* class but differ in the rather more British style of plated-in stern.

The superstructure has a compact appearance. There is no separate funnel, the capped uptakes being integral with the bridge structure. This is topped-off by a light pole mast which looks fragile in comparison with the mass of antennae that it supports. These include a 3-D unit giving both

No. PA54/R98 *Clemenceau*

heights and ranges to the SENIT automatic tactical data system. Surveillance antennae are adjacent and the dome at the after end of the island shrouds an aircraft approach control radar.

The flight deck is armoured and pierced by two elevators. One of these is side-mounted, American style, to starboard abaft the island with the other forward of it on the centreline.

About 40 aircraft are normally carried, usually a mix of Dassault Etandard IV fighter-bomber/interceptors, F-8E Crusader fighters, Breguet Alize AS aircraft and utility helicopters. Additional AS potency is given by an American-pattern hull mounted sonar, working with dunked or aircraft-laid sonars via the SENIT to direct attacking aircraft.

For a navy as missile-minded as the French, it is surprising that the defensive armament is still all-gun, disposed in eight single 100mm-mountings. They are automatic, dual-purpose weapons with a high rate of fire of about 60 rounds per minute.

Stability may have been a problem, as the second to be completed, *Foch,* was widened by bulges during construction. *Clemenceau* had hers fitted later.

A new 18,000-ton nuclear propelled carrier is to be laid down in 1975. Comparable in size and functions with the British *Invincible* (q.v.) she will operate helicopters and probably S/VTOL aircraft.

PH 75 Project Nuclear Propelled Helicopter Carrier   France

Data (Provisional) No. R75 No name yet known
Laid Down: 1976
Launched: 1978
Completed: 1980
Displacement: 18,500 Deep Load
Length (o.a.): 682ft
Beam: 87ft
(Width over flight deck 81ft)
Machinery: one nuclear reactor and two geared steam turbine sets. Two shafts 64,000 shp for 28 knots
Armament: Two octal CROTALE SAM launchers. Eight 40mm AA guns (initially)
Helicopters: 12 heavy or 25 light or combination V/STOL capable

With the retirement of the ex-British Colossus-class *Arromanches* in 1974, the French Navy was left with only the training cruiser *Jeanne d'Arc* to operate in a pure helicopter-carrying role. Preliminary details have been released regarding the former ship's replacement, which will not enter service until the early 'eighties. With no requirement for the large carriers of the super powers, the French have taken the adventurous technological decision of putting a nuclear reactor into a modest-sized hull. This installation provides steam via a heat exchanger to two conventional steam turbine sets, each driving a shaft. In the event of a reactor shut-down, the ship can still be propelled at 10 knots by a pair of 'get-you-home' diesels of comparatively low power.

In appearance, the ship resembles an escort carrier of World War II, with her boxy, funnel-less island and single large mast, but there the parallel

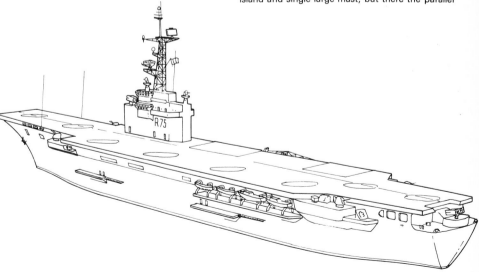

and single large mast, but there the parallel ends. She is, like the escort carrier, designed basically for area defence with little strike capability. There is no angled deck or arrestor gear and the usual aircraft complement will be of helicopters whose mix will depend on the particular mission being pursued. There is every intention, however, of eventually shipping a section of V/STOL aircraft in addition.

The ship carries accommodation and facilities for up to 1,500 troops and can put them ashore with their equipment either with large SA 321 Super Frelon helicopters or LCA's carried under davits. Personnel can be embarked via sideports and heavy gear loaded by the fixed crane, which can plumb either of the two side elevators on the starboard side abaft the island. There is a vehicle deck forward of the hangar but as there is no capacity for trans-shipping heavy armour, the ship would need to work as part of a task group for extended amphibious operations.

The helicopters, primarily the smaller SA330 Pumas or WG 13 Lynxs, provide the A/S cover necessary with the ship's hull-mounted sonar and central facilities co-ordinating operations. A/A defence is covered by two Crotale systems, whose eight-celled launchers are mounted atop the island forward of the bridge and right aft. Initially 40mm guns will be provided on quarter sponsons, but these will eventually be replaced by point-defence missile systems with anti-missile capability.

Although the helicopters can carry anti-ship missiles, it is in this sphere that the design is weak and escorts will need to be provided. As they cannot match the range of their charge the latter has bunkers for some 1,200 tons of fuel, which can be transfered whilst under weigh.

Radar facilities are comprehensive including the rectangular antenna of a DRBV 51 air/surface search set atop the mast and the elliptical DRBV 26 air search scanner on the forward side. Two small towers support the separate DRBC 32 Crotale guidance antennas.

Jeanne d'Arc Helicopter Cruiser

France

Units: No. R97 *Jeanne d'Arc* (ex-*La Resolue*)
Laid Down: 1960
Launched: 1961
Completed: 1964
Displacement: 10,000 standard
12,400 Deep Load
Length (o.a.): 597ft
Beam: 79ft
Draught: 24ft
Machinery: Geared steam turbines 2 shafts
40,000shp for 26½ knots
Helicopters: Six — Exocet SSM launchers (2 × 3)
Maximum 8 large
Armament: Four — 3.9-inch (4 × 1)

France is one of the few naval powers that designs specialised training ships. Completed in 1963, the present ship bears the name of a predecessor which dated from 1931. With the armament and much of the appearance of contemporary French cruisers, this ship differed by incorporating what were virtually promenade decks opening off spacious accommodation for about 180 personnel undergoing sea training.

Obsolete by the 'fifties, she was due for replacement by more modern tonnage and so closely associated had her name and function become that it was decided to rename the replacement *Jeanne d'Arc* also. As she was completed before the decommissioning of her predecessor, she took the temporary name of *La Resolue* until her proper name became available.

Built under the 1957 estimates, the ship was of entirely novel design, anticipating the broadly similar Russian *Moskva* by several years. The design has not been developed any further by the French although it has influenced several navies in the layout of hybrid helicopter cruisers. Basically she is a cruiser forward, equipped with full command facilities, with a flight deck overlaying a hangar aft.

A handsome ship, the forecastle deck rises one level to the flight deck, at the forward end of which is a centreline island superstructure. This is a compact affair with a wide spacious wheelhouse, boasting an expanse of glazing well up to mercantile practice and giving excellent visibility in all directions although vulnerable to blast.

On the same deck at the after end of the island is the complementary set of windows of the helicopter flight control room which is laid out around the uptake casing leading to the funnel directly above. This latter is nicely proportioned and replaces an earlier smaller funnel which proved unequal to the task of carrying exhaust gases clear of the complex eddy systems formed by the bridge mass. This is a common failing which often can be cured in the design stage by wind-tunnel experiments on a model.

Forward of the funnel is a tall, tapered pole mast which, with its antennae, is strongly akin to that on a *Clemenceau*.

The flight deck extends some 200 feet aft from the island, dropping two decks to the quarterdeck. On the centreline at this change of level is an elevator capable of moving the largest seaborne helicopters between hangar and flightdeck. Up to eight of these can be housed in the central hangar which is flanked by two-decked accommodation for nearly 200 cadets.

Radar, although comprehensive, is not on the same scale as on the specialist aircraft carriers. Hull mounted sonar is fitted, giving backup to the sets installed in the helicopters. This enables co-ordinates to be given for a directed attack with AS torpedoes. As an alternative, the helicopters can carry the AS12 air-to-surface missile. This is a small visually guided missile with a range of about 4 miles. It is widely used and very effective against smaller craft.

Ship's armament was all-gun, with four single 100mm weapons being sided aft and forward with rather restricted firing arcs. She has now (1975) been fitted with two triple Exocet SAM launchers forward of the bridge. As an assault ship, she can carry the equipment and personnel of a full battalion.

Colbert Guided Missile Cruiser
France

Units: No. C611 *Colbert*
Laid Down: 1953
Launched: 1956
Completed: 1959
Displacement: 8,500 standard
11,300 Deep Load
Length (o.a.): 593ft
Beam: 65ft
Draught: 25ft
Machinery: Geared steam turbines 2 shafts
86,000shp for 32 knots
Armament: Two—Masurca launchers (1 × 2)
Two—3.9-inch (100mm) DP guns (2 × 1)
Twelve—57mm AA guns (6 × 2)

Laid down in 1953, *Colbert* is a near sister of *De Grasse* which was disposed of in 1973. Commenced before World War II the latter was not complete until 1956, followed in 1959 by *Colbert*. Both were armed as anti-aircraft cruisers but, by the time that *Colbert* was designed, it had already been obvious that the guided missile was set to oust the gun as a primary weapon. The hull, therefore, was laid out with an eye to a future major conversion.

Both ships were heavier Gallic equivalents to the American *Juneaus*. They had a main battery of no less than sixteen 5-inch guns in eight twin mountings. Four were disposed 'normally' in superfiring 'A', 'B', 'X' and 'Y' positions with the other four in sided pairs abaft 'B' and forward of 'X'.

Grouped around the superstructure were ten more large powered turrets, each containing a pair of 57mm weapons. This total of eighteen mountings gave a not unpleasing 'bristling' appearance to the ship.

The profile broke the tradition of twin funnelled French cruisers, with a single vertical stack surmounted by a distinctive funnel cap.

The bridge mass was square and compact, but the overall cleanness of the design was marred by a pair of lattice masts located betwixt funnel and bridge.

The hull was clean with slight sheer and a high freeboard amidships where the superstructure was taken, unusually, right out to the side of the ship over most of its length, broken only by a small boat aperture.

The option on missiles was taken up in 1970, when *Colbert* entered Brest Naval Dockyard for a two-year reconstruction. With the exception of six twin 57mm mountings in the waist, the complete original gun armament was stripped out being replaced, in 'A' and 'B' positions only, by automatic single DP 100mm turrets.

Appearance was improved by the removal of the lattice mast immediately forward of the funnel, the position of the large antenna of the 3-D radar being moved further aft.

In the 'Y' position is now sited a twin Masurca SAM launcher with its twin directors forward of it. This is a system with a range of something over 20 miles with missiles guided by radar, although later versions have semi-active homing heads to improve performance in the final stage against the targets ECM devices.

It was announced during the reconstruction that

Colbert would have up to four Exocet SSM launchers fitted in addition, but these have not materialised. She is therefore, rather deficient in surface weaponry but the clue to justify this lies in the unusually comprehensive radar fit. Both *Colbert* and her near sister were built with command facilities and their role is primarily one of direction, thus the weapon fit is defensive rather than offensive.

The broader transom stern of the later ship has enabled provision to be made for a helicopter although no hangar has been supplied. As a hull-mounted sonar is included it could be inferred that the helicopter could carry AS torpedoes.

The age and more intricate sub-division of *De Grasse* militated against a similar conversion.

Suffren Guided Missile Destroyer France

Units: No. D602 *Suffren*
No. D603 *Duquesne*

	Suffren	Duquesne
Laid Down:	1962	1964
Launched:	1965	1966
Completed:	1967	1970

Displacement: 5,100 standard
6,100 Deep Load
Length (o.a.): 517ft
Beam: 51ft
Draught: 20ft
Machinery: Geared steam turbines 2 shafts
72,500shp for 34 knots
Armament: Two—3.9-inch (100mm) guns
(2 × 1)
Two—30mm AA guns (2 × 1)
One—Twin Masurca SA launcher
One—Malafon rocket launcher for As torpedoes
Four—AS torpedo tubes (2 × 2)

An impressively handsome pair of ships, the *Suffrens* have a truly Gallic dash of eccentricity with an enormous radome covering the 3-D antenna and giving a profile unique amongst destroyers. For size, the most immediate comparison is with the Russian *Kresta I* type although the weapon fit falls far short. The appearance is much more balanced, lacking the agressiveness of the Soviet design.

Suffren, laid down in 1962, represented a new departure in French naval design. Previously construction had been divided clearly between the classic multi-purpose destroyer layouts of the *Surcoufs* and various escorts with clearly defined functions. An attempt was first made here to provide a multi-function escort, built around available guided weapon systems. Unlike the Russians, the French made no attempt to cram anti-surface, AA and AS missilry into one hull.

Thus, the surface armament is still a pair of well-tried 100mm DP guns although, had it been available, the compact Exocet might well have been fitted.

The above-decks layout looks like influencing a whole series of subsequent French flotilla classes. Most obvious innovation is the 'mack' or mast/stack combination. Hot stack gases in the presence of the salty atmosphere are exceedingly corrosive

No. D602 *Suffren*

on masthead fittings, particularly antennae. The latter, moreover, require a vibration-free environment where possible, which calls for a stiff mounting structure. The mack is therefore, a rational approach with electronics atop a tubular tower inside which the leads can be taken with resultant protection from splinter damage. Also led up this structure are the engine and boiler room exhausts which vent on either side, well clear of vulnerable fittings. The combination also saves deck space and topweight, both vital considerations in a small complex ship. The French have also a flair for making a potentially ugly fitting into a distinctive feature.

A twin launcher for Masurca SAM's is sited on the low quarterdeck with a pair of DRBR 51 directors immediately forward of it.

As no provision has been made for a helicopter, AS capability rests heavily on the Malafon launcher amidships. This is a complex weapon of 10 miles range consisting of a homing AS torpedo carried as part of a winged body which is rocket-fired towards a submarine target. Updated information is fed in to its flight system during passage and the torpedo is jettisoned short of the target, thence homing normally. Sonar is incorporated in both the hull and a VDS set which partially compensates for the lack of a helicopter.

A pair of AS torpedo tubes can be sided in the waist for use against close-range targets.

As in major units of the French Navy, a SENIT automatic tactical data system has been fitted permitting the free interchange of information between the various ships comprising a task group.

Boat stowage is interesting, small craft laying in a protected position abaft the bridge and handled by a powered crane in preference to davits.

Propulsion is conventionally by steam turbine, the French not being so enthusiastic about the gas turbine as are other navies.

Tourville Guided Missile Destroyer   France

Units: No. D610 *Tourville* (ex-No. F604)
No. D611 *Duguay-Trouin* (ex-No. F605)
D612 *De Grasse* (ex-No. F606)

	Tourville	Duguay-Trouin	De Grasse
Laid Down:	1970	1971	1972
Launched:	1972	1973	1974
Completed:	1974	1974	1975

Displacement: 4,600 standard
5,750 Deep Load
Length (o.a.): 510ft
Beam: 50ft
Draught: 19ft
Machinery: Geared steam turbines 2 shafts
55,000shp for 32 knots
Armament: Three—3.9-inch (100mm) guns
(3 × 1)
Two—Triple Exocet SSM launchers
One—Malafon rocket launcher for torpedoes
Two—AS torpedo tubes (2 × 1)
Helicopters: Two WG13 Lynx. Hangar

This trio was originally designated Type C67, being a design development of the Type C65 *Aconit;* being somewhat enlarged, however, the term 'corvette' was less than correct so that they were reclassed Type F67 (frigate) with a final touch of eccentricity conferred by the destroyers 'D' pennant number.

The design is really a variant on the earlier *Suffrens* with its AA capability reduced in favour of a greater surface armament. Similar in appearance at first sight, the *Tourvilles* can be identified by the lack of a SAM launcher and directors aft. This space is utilised for a hangar and flightdeck for a pair of Lynx helicopters, which more than rectifies the omission of one in the *Suffrens*.

This is achieved on a shorter hull and lower tonnage than those of the earlier class and basically by virtue of the adoption of the Exocet as the SSM. The launchers for these are compact enough to be mounted quite high amidships, saving valuable end space in the hull. A triple launcher is mounted on either side abaft the bridge and angled out from the ship's longitudinal axis. A limited training arc is built in, easing gathering problems if the ship cannot change course during an attack.

The Exocet missiles are controlled by two radars, the large DRBV-26 antenna on the 'mack' giving long-range surveillance whilst target designation and tracking are performed via the DRBV-51 on the stump lattice foremast. This will eventually be covered by a protective GRP dome similar to that on the Suffrens.

Exocets are low level SSMs effective out to about 20 miles and not intended for use against aircraft and, without the larger ship's Masurca SAM system, AA defence depends on DP guns. There are three 100mm automatic single mountings fitted, the extra one being located in a rather odd position high up on the forward end of the hangar roof. The third unit, *De Grasse*, will be fitted with an octal Crotale SAM launcher in place of the after gun. Crotale is a compact short range (5 miles) missile roughly equivalent to the British Seacat.

AS capacity is considerable. A Malafon missile/ torpedo is mounted in a sheltered position amidships and there are two launchers for L5 homing torpedoes. Attack information comes from either of the two shipborne sonar sets, one in a bow bulb and the other in a VDS unit which can be streamed from right aft. Additional data can be added from the dunked sonars of the two Lynx helicopters, being processed and forwarded by the ship's SENIT system. The helicopters can themselves attack a submerged target with the lightweight L6 homer.

Alternatively they can deploy four AS12 air-to-surface missiles, giving the ship a long range capacity against surface targets, with the missile-armed FPB particularly in mind.

Even though the ship is propelled by 'conventional' steam turbines, the French have succeeded

in reducing the crew by over 25%, compared with the marginally larger *Suffrens,* to just over 300 total.

The class would probably have run to many more than three had not it been decided to 'go gas-turbine'. A new design, known as the C70 corvette is therefore due to enter service about 1978 and run to over 20 units in total.

Ouragan Landing Ship (Dock)   France

Units: No. L9021 *Ouragan*
No. L9022 *Orage*

	Ouragan	Orage
Laid Down:	1962	1966
Launched:	1963	1967
Completed:	1964	1968

Displacement: 5,800 standard
8,500 Deep Load
Length (o.a.): 489ft
Beam: 71ft
Draught: 16ft
Machinery: Twin diesels on 2 shafts
8,700shp for 17 knots
Armament: Two — 120mm mortars
Six — 30mm AA

Experience with LSD operation was gained by the French through the loan of the ex-American *Cabildo*-class *Foudre*. Built for the US Navy as LSD 12 she was transferred to Britain in 1944 as the *Oceanway*. Subsequently hoisting the Greek flag, she served as their *Okeanos* until 1952. The French then retained her until 1969, by which time two home-designed ships had been commissioned.

Although these are rather smaller than later designs commissioned into the US and British fleets they must inevitably be compared with them. The overall sterngate principle is similar with the most important design variation visible externally through the stumpy funnels, the ships being diesel-propelled. As a type, the LSD has a sea speed rarely exceeding 20 knots; the French, by

accepting a slightly lower speed of 17 knots as adequate, produced a design that could be propelled by less than 9,000shp. This was easily within the capabilities of two comparatively small diesels, particularly as French designs for medium speed types are renowned and widely used commercially.

This style of engine has a high power to weight ratio and is used in the LSD for the same reason as in many car ferries, i.e. a low profile. This characteristic enables it to be fitted below a vehicle deck, which can then have a clear run without obstructions.

Another plus for the diesel is its economy of operation, giving the range so vital to a warship. As oil fuel becomes ever more expensive and scarce, it may well be that the diesel is more widely accepted in warship propulsion, particularly as displacements have tended to decrease together with requirements for high speed. This latter point is now more common as the helicopter increasingly acts as a rapid extension to a ship's armament.

The *Ouragans* are equipped with a squared-off, rather featureless bridge, topped with a simple pole mast and reminiscent of WW II escort carriers. This impression is intensified by its being offset as an island structure to starboard of a small flight deck of dimensions suitable for handling up to four large helicopters, which would perform a vital role in achieving a rapid establishment ashore. This flight deck is the roof of a large storage area for vehicles or wheeled supplies. A walkway with apertures

No. L9021 *Ouragan*

runs along its length on either side for rapid movement of troops to the helicopters. Up to 500 troops can be transported over short distances.

The dock can accommodate craft as large as EDIC's—the French equivalent of an LCT—two of which can be stowed in line. Better space utilisation is achieved by loading LCM's, of which a dozen of the French CTM type can be accommodated. These are craft of over 90 feet in length and stowing about 100 tons of cargo. They would normally be loaded before floating in but would need reloading during the course of a landing. To facilitate this, two conspicuous 35-ton cranes are sided and are able to plump craft both in the dock or alongside.

Small LCA type craft can also be used to supplement the force; these are stowed on a movable platform spanning the after end of the dock and are also handled by the cranes.

Armament and radars are on a light scale as the ships are not designed for a command role. *Ouragan* has a hull mounted sonar set which suggests that her helicopters could be used in an AS capacity.

Deutschland Training Ship   West Germany

Units: No. A59 *Deutschland*
Laid Down: 1959
Launched: 1960
Completed: 1963
Displacement: 4,900 standard
5,500 Deep Load
Length (o.a.): 476ft
Beam: 52.5ft
Draught: 16ft
Machinery: One geared steam turbine 8,000shp
Two Maybach + Two MAN diesels—Total 6,700shp
Total SHP 14,700shp 22 knots 3 shafts
Armament: Four—3.9-inch (4 × 1)
Six—40mm (2 × 2) and (2 × 1)
Four—AS TT
Two—Surface TT
Two—4-barrelled AS Rocket Launchers

This vessel of highly interesting design fits into the 'major warship' category only by virtue of her tonnage. Intended as a pure training ship, she was to have been named *Berlin*, but this was changed to the more prestigious *Deutschland* before her launch. This name is more suited to her role which shows the West German flag throughout the world.

Launched fifteen years after the end of WW II she was the first German warship to exceed the postwar limitation of 3,000 tons. No attempt was made to make her other than a training ship and so, for her tonnage, her silhouette is much too large and her armament far too small. The overall dimensions are largely accounted for by the accommodation for some 250 cadets who can 'work the ship' in all departments to gain practical experience at sea.

Thus, one feature—almost unique in a ship of this size—is a triple shaft arrangement.

The wing shafts are each powered by two diesels and, of the total of four, two are of Maybach manufacture and two of Mercedes-Benz. Both of these marques are common in the Bundesmarine and experience can thus be gained on either type. The centre shaft is driven by a rather low power steam turbine built by MAN, a firm more associated with diesels. The steam for this unit is raised in a pair of Wahodag boilers, the usual choice in the fleet. Frigates of the *Köln* class have CODAG propulsion and experience in this system must be gained elsewhere as no gas turbines are carried.

The small surface armament consists only of four 100mm (3.9-inch) guns, which are spaced-out in single mountings to train as many crews as possible, simultaneously. They are DP weapons and fire control is from a Hollandse Signaal Apparaten director. This director controls also the AA armament of six 40mm weapons, split between two twin and two single mountings. The Dutch firm supplied also all radars and fire controls for the varied AS armament.

The main AS weapons are the two four-barrelled Bofors rocket launchers, firing on forward arcs from a position superior to 'B' gun. Four AS torpedo tubes are carried, these in addition to a further couple for surface use.

No helicopter is carried, but the wide, un-cluttered quarterdeck is well capable of handling one, although no covered accommodation could be provided.

For her modest size, this many-tiered ship looks quite impressive but her role in the event of hostilities would be difficult to define. She would most likely be employed as a Headquarters Ship where her low speed would not be too inhibiting a factor and her capacious accommodation a great advantage.

She exhibits many recognition features typical of German warships; among them, the large funnel with prominent black cap, a pronounced knuckle in the hull with anchor pocket set high against the sheer-strake.

Her 'A' pennant number proclaims her auxiliary status.

Nafkratoussa Landing Ship Dock

Greece

Units: L153 *Nafkratoussa* (ex-USS *Fort Mandan*, LSD 21)
Laid Down: 1945
Launched: 1945
Completed: 1945
Displacement: 4,800 light
9,400 Deep Load
Length (o.a.): 458ft
Beam: 72ft
Draught: 18ft
Machinery: Geared steam turbines 2 shafts
7,000shp for 15 knots
Armament: 8 × 40mm
Capacity: 18 LCM (Landing Craft, Mechanised) or
3 LCU (Landing Craft, Utility) or
32 LVT (Tractors, amphibious)
For others of this class, see:
Galicia (Spain)

The 'army' war in the Pacific, 1941-5, was essentially one of disputed islands. Equipped harbours were rare and the Americans reacted very quickly in producing a multitude of landing craft types to deliver men and material 'over the beach'. These craft were generally small, simple and expendable, very limited in range and seagoing capabilities. With the vast distances involved, it was essential that these small craft be attended or transported by mother ships. Initially, these were converted merchantmen but, at best, they could accommodate only those assault landing craft small enough to be housed in davits.

Getting heavy armour, earth-moving equipment, etc., ashore needed a different solution and the Landing Ship, Dock was evolved.

The first group of these was the *Ashland* class; built rapidly and incorporating available reciprocating machinery, they were commissioned 1943-4. More compact machinery was required, however, and the second group, the *Cabildos,* were steam turbine propelled.

A unit of the first type (ex-LSD-9) was transferred to the Hellenic Navy in 1953 as amphibious headquarters ship. Named *Nafkratoussa* she served under the Greek flag until 1971 when she was replaced by a unit of the later, similar-sized class. Taking the same name, she had been the LSD 21.

Both classes were of small ships, with a standard tonnage under 5,000 but they were of revolutionary design, being a hybrid ship-cum-floating dock.

As evinced by the close similarity of all later classes, their design was sound. The after two-thirds was a U-section floating dock and the forward one-third a conventional ship, the forecastle deck of which extended aft to form a bridge over the forward part of the dock. This deck was extended upwards to form a long low two-deck superstructure with a bridge and various other erections on top.

In operation, water is admitted to the dock area, trimming the ship by the stern until, with a small freeboard still remaining, the water levels in and outside the transom dockgate are equalised. This gate then hinges downwards giving free passage

for small craft in or out of the dock area. Movements completed, the gate is raised and secured and the water inside pumped out. As the ship rises in the water the small craft inside are left high and dry.

Uptakes from the machinery are necessarily split and run up either side of the dock area to avoid casings impinging on cargo space. Modern ferries use the same technique to avoid obstacles on car decks.

The forward end of the dock area is permanently bridged by the superstructure but the after end was left open to the sky to give headroom for embarked craft having a substantial air draught.

A temporary deck can be fitted over this area when possible, acting as a useful helicopter pad and thus enabling discharge to be effected more efficiently.

The island-studded Greek waters have much in common with the Pacific and, for its size, the Hellenic Navy has a large force of amphibious ships including over 50 LCM's, LCU's and LCVP's, any of which can be transportable by *Nafkratoussa*.

Vikrant Aircraft Carrier   India

Units: No. R11 *Vikrant* (ex-HMS *Hercules*)
Laid Down: 1943
Launched: 1945
Completed: 1961
Displacement: 16,000 standard
19,500 Deep Load
Length (o.a.): 700ft
Beam: 80ft
Draught: 24ft
Machinery: Geared steam turbines 2 shafts
40,000shp for 24½ knots
Armament: Fifteen—40mm (4 × 2) + (7 × 1)
For others of this class, see:
25 de Mayo   (Argentina)
Minas Gerais (Brazil)
Melbourne   (Australia)

A unit of the British *Majestic* class of Light Fleet Carrier, *Vikrant* started life as HMS *Hercules*.

Although rushed towards completion, none of the six was ready for service at the war's end although too far advanced to be economically scrapped. All were launched and laid up incomplete, pending the formulation of a postwar policy for the RN. Austerity measures forced a drastic culling of fleet strength and many units were scrapped, transferred or sold. Of the *Majestics,* two each went to Australia and Canada. The remaining pair were *Leviathan* and *Hercules.* The former lay for years at Portsmouth acting as a store and was cannibalised extensively for spare parts.

In the late 'fifties a plan was announced for enlarging the Indian Flotilla to the Indian Fleet. The UK was to supply modern ships and the emergent navy would then be charged with the responsible task of the defence of the sub-continent's massive coastline.

Air reconnaissance and strike capability would

clearly be needed and, in 1957, the transfer of *Hercules* was announced.

Launched on the Tyne and laid-up in Scotland for over a decade, she was towed to Belfast for completion. This took four years and she was commissioned in 1961 as INS *Vikrant* with the, by now, standard angled deck and steam catapult.

Still very much a British carrier in appearance, she varied visually from the rest of the class through the light aerial mast atop the bridge and forward of the mainmast. Internally she was improved by partial air conditioning and thermal insulation. The crew of over 1,300 have much improved accommodation to that provided in the standard war-built carriers.

Although the hull is now quite aged, the machinery is comparatively new. What had happened before her completion was a rapid increase in the size and weight of strike aircraft and the make-up of the air wing aboard is rather mixed.

Without modern long-range search radar *Vikrant* must depend greatly upon the reconnaissance facilities provided by her embarked Grumman S2-A *Trackers.* AS strikes were dependent upon a dozen Breguet Alize aircraft, which would need sonobuoys or co-operation from an escort ship for attack, as their carrier does not have a hull sonar.

Surface strikes are still furnished by the venerable Sea Hawks with which she was originally equipped. These may well be past their best by modern major power standards but the influence they exerted in the Indo-Pakistan War of 1971 shows that, for a limited war, less sophisticated weaponry is still effective. It underlines the undeniable precept that, in a sea war, any aircraft are better than no aircraft.

The escalating size of carriers is being halted by the general use of the helicopter and by the likely adoption of the V/STOL aircraft. Thus, the *Vikrant's* Alizes are likely to yield place to SH-3 Sea Kings and the Sea Hawks to either the Sea Harrier or by the Russian Yak equivalent known as Freehand — if it is made available. The Indians have demonstrated already that they are ready to turn to the Eastern Bloc for military supplies should they not be readily forthcoming from more traditional sources.

Mysore Light Cruiser   India

Units: No. C60 *Mysore* (ex-HMS *Nigeria*)
Laid Down: 1938
Launched: 1939
Completed: 1940
Displacement: 8,700 standard
11,000 Deep Load
Length (o.a.): 555ft
Beam: 62ft
Draught: 21ft
Machinery: Geared steam turbines 4 shafts 72,000shp for 31 knots
Armament: Nine—6-inch (3 × 3)
Eight—4-inch (4 × 2)
Twelve—40mm (5 × 2) + (2 × 1)

For others of the class, see:
  Capitan Quiñones } Peru
  Coronel Bolognesi }

The strongly 'perpendicular' appearance of *Mysore* betrays immediately her origins as an ex-British war-emergency cruiser. She was a unit of the first group, the *Crown Colony* or *Fiji* class. They were a direct and more austere derivative of the handsome *Southamptons* of 1937 of which none now remains. These were a most successful design, rather larger than earlier RN light cruiser groups which are now represented only by such veterans as *Delhi* and *La Argentina.* Fast and well armed with twelve 6-inch guns of proven performance, the major drawback in design lay in its expense and it did not lend itself to rapid series production.

Thus, when, with war looming, a spate of warship orders was placed the design was modified to become the *Fiji* class. The same armament was retained but, externally, the graceful rake of funnels and masts gave way to to the business-like verticality which is such a strong feature.

The cruiser stern was superseded by the squared-off transom which was then becoming general. This reduced vibration considerably besides producing a shorter hull.

The class of eight was very heavily worked during WW II and was fortunate in losing only two of its number. Modern cruisers were still useful units after the war and few were disposed of, finding their old employment along the Imperial searoutes. Politics and patterns of trade were changing rapidly, however, and an impoverished UK imposed a series of cuts on its fleet strength, with many fine ships going under foreign flags.

As part of the building-up of the Indian Fleet, HMS *Nigeria* found herself the first *Fiji* to be 'sold out', becoming the *Mysore* in 1954. Her RN war service had taken her to the Arctic and Norway and thence to the Mediterranean where she was damaged by a torpedo whilst forming part of the screen on the famous 'August Convoy' to Malta.

It was not until 1957 that she was delivered to India, having undergone a thorough refit and modernisation. The proliferation of retro-fitted radars and other assorted topweight resulted in most British cruisers losing their X-turret to compensate. Of this group, *Nigeria* had been the only unit to retain it, but it was finally replaced by two twin 40mm mountings during modernisation. A feature of the 6-inch turret is that the centre gun is set back slightly to reduce interaction of shells when adjacent guns are fired simultaneously.

More saving in topweight was effected by the landing of aircraft and catapults together with the two triple 21-inch torpedo tubes, although this was sacrificed as a result of policy rather than for stability considerations. The aircraft crane was retained for boat-handling purposes.

The old tripod masts were no longer of sufficient strength to support the growing weight of electronics and they were replaced by rather inelegant lattice masts.

Director controls were also improved; the four twin 4-inch HA mountings grouped abaft the after funnel gained Mark VI 'greenhouses' sided above what had been the aircraft hangars.

Now 36 years of age, her useful range may justify some more years of life on a coastline more than 2,500 miles in length.

Delhi Light Cruiser   India

Units: No. C74 *Delhi* (ex-HMS *Achilles*)
Laid Down: 1931
Launched: 1932
Completed: 1933
Displacement: 7,100 standard
9,700 Deep Load
Length (o.a.): 555ft
Beam: 55ft
Draught: 20ft
Machinery: Geared steam turbines 4 shafts
72,000shp for 32 knots
Armament: Six—6-inch (3 × 2)
Eight—4-inch (4 × 2)
Fourteen—40mm (4 × 2) + (6 × 1)

Now over 40 years old and reduced to a training role, *Delhi's* continued existence owes much to a single day in her career when, as HMNZS *Achilles,* she was one of the trio of cruisers that outfought the *Graf Spee* off the Plate Estuary in December 1939.

Laid down at Birkenhead in 1931, she was completed in 1933 as one of the quintet of *Leander* class light cruisers (not to be confused with the present-day frigates of that name). They were the first of the type to be constructed since the C & D types of World War I and marked a reversion to the light cruiser at a time when most navies were building to the maximum size permitted by the Washington Treaty.

Handsome, symmetrical little ships, their profile was enhanced by the trunked Italianate funnel. This feature, however, reflected a weakness of the design in that it is was possible only through close-spacing of boiler rooms. This is not good practice in a warship—one hit can immobilise the whole steam plant—and the derivative classes (*Amphions* and *Arethusas*) had their boiler rooms much more

widely spaced resulting in a distinctive but less handsome pair of funnels with a wide gap between (see *La Argentina*, a very similar ship).

Although much lighter in appearance, *Delhi* is, surprisingly, only marginally shorter than her running mate, *Mysore* and it says much for design improvements that the latter could deploy twelve 6-inch guns compared with the earlier class's eight. An extra seven feet beam was required but, with the same power, as speed penalty of only a half-knot was incurred.

Together with her sister, *Leander,* the *Achilles* was serving as part of the Royal New Zealand Navy at the outbreak of World War II and, after repair of damage sustained at the Plate, she returned to the Pacific. She spent the greater part of the war in these waters, returning to the UK briefly in 1943 for a new turret to replace one destroyed by Japanese bombing off Guadalcanal.

After the war, her three surviving sisters were scrapped, but *Achilles* was modified by the removal of her X-turret and augmentation of her 40mm AA armament. Addition of search and gunnery radars had already necessitated the replacement of the earlier pole masts by tripods but, fortunately from the appearance aspect, these were not in turn superseded by the in-vogue lattice type. This was because she was not extensively modernised, being transferred to India in 1948.

Along with other British cruisers, she lost her catapult and aircraft soon after the war and the later deletion of two quadruple banks of torpedo tubes (sided one level down abaft the funnel) resulted in the side plating being continued farther aft, creating more accommodation and a heavier appearance to the hull.

Delhi served as flagship to the Indian Navy until the arrival of *Mysore* and even in her present function as training ship, it is difficult to see her serving much longer, with spares becoming more of a problem. As she is little-changed from her original appearance it would be good to see her eventually preserved in the fashion of the *Belfast*.

Until recently a minor, small ship navy, the Iranian fleet is now set to become a major Middle-Eastern force. Six *Spruance*-class destroyers (q.v.) have been ordered from the US (1974) and interest has been reported in an AS cruiser of the British *Invincible* type (q.v.). The establishment of a submarine arm could include nuclear units should they be available.

Iran

Until recently a minor, small ship navy, the Iranian fleet is now set to become a major Middle-Eastern force. Four *Spruance*-class destroyers (q.v.) have been ordered from the US (1976) and interest has been reported in an A/S cruiser of the British *Invincible* type (q.v.). The establishment of a submarine arm could include nuclear units should they be available.

Vittorio Veneto Helicopter Cruiser   Italy

Units: No. C550 *Vittorio Veneto*
Laid Down: 1965
Launched: 1967
Completed: 1969
Displacement: 7,500 standard
8,400 Deep Load
Length (o.a.): 558ft
Beam: 64ft
Draught: 17ft
Machinery: Geared steam turbines 2 shafts
73,000shp for 32 knots
Armament: One — Twin launcher for Terrier/Asroc missiles
Eight — 3-inch DP automatic guns (8 × 1)
Six — 12-inch AS torpedo tubes (2 × 3)
Helicopters: Nine Agusta-Bell 240B

Italy has been responsible for much innovation in warship design, particularly in the cruiser category. In 1964 were completed the two *Andrea Dorias* (q.v.), fine ships which greatly influenced a pair of enlarged designs which were due to follow on. One of these was to be another cruiser with enhanced helicopter stowage and a capacity for amphibious assault. She was to have been named *Italia* but the project was delayed, the design modified and the name changed to *Trieste*. As such, the project lingered until 1968 before being cancelled for lack of funds.

A second design was for a simpler ship, again an enlarged helicopter carrying cruiser with a single-ended missile armament. She was laid down in 1965 as the *Vittorio Veneto* but, as operational experience was now becoming available from the *Dorias*, the design was recast several times and her completion in under four years was quite a creditable achievement. Her nearest counterpart is the much larger Russian *Moskva* (q.v.) commissioned a couple of years earlier. France's *Jeanne d'Arc* (q.v.) is closer in size but her general concept is geared more closely to a command role than the more offensive cruiser design of the Italians. There are, nevertheless, similarities in the layout with a nicely sheered, knuckled forecastle rising one level to the bridge and continuing aft to the flight deck. There is a flat run aft giving broad sections for the flight deck which thus has a good width without the adoption of excessive flare used, for instance, in the British *Tiger* conversions.

Vittorio Veneto is of much higher power than

Jeanne d'Arc necessitating more boiler spaces and two funnels. The latter dictate that the superstructure has more of a traditional cruiser layout than that in the French ship.

The potentially stiff tower structures of the funnel casings have been well used as low-vibration mountings for the major antennae. The uptakes are brought up the inside and exhaust via angled vents near the top, the corrosive gases being carried clear.

Atop the large, square bridge are the two American SPG-55 directors associated with the twin missile launcher in 'A' position. This is one of the dual-function types which can launch either Terrier (AA) or Asroc (AS) missiles. It backs on to a low structure extending forward of the bridge and containing the magazine and complex loading arrangements demanded by the twin functions.

Search and aerial targetting for the Terrier system is performed by an American SPS-48 3-D system, whose square antenna is prominent on the forward mack.

Information for the Asroc or the six AS torpedo tubes is supplied from either the hull-mounted sonar or from dipping units operated by any of the ship's nine helicopters.

These are Agusta-Bell 240B AS types which can all be accommodated below the rectangular flight deck which extends right aft to the transom. There is a lift at the forward end and space abaft this for five pads.

Surface armament consists of only eight 3-inch guns, which are disposed in single, automatic DP mountings.

A large number of inflatable rafts are racked at the after end of the superstructure, suggesting that a military force could be transported over a limited range.

Andrea Doria Helicopter Cruiser   Italy

Units: No. C553 *Andrea Doria* (ex-*Enrico Dandolo*)
No. C554 *Caio Duilio*

	Andrea Doria	Caio Duilio
Laid Down:	1958	1958
Launched:	1963	1962
Completed:	1964	1964

Displacement: 5,000 standard
6,500 Deep Load
Length (o.a.): 490ft

Beam: 56ft
Draught: 17ft
Machinery: Geared steam turbines 2 shafts 60,000shp for 30 knots
Armament: One—Twin launcher for Terrier missiles
Eight—3-inch DP automatic guns
Six—12-inch AS torpedo tubes (2 × 3)
Helicopters: Four Agusta-Bell 240B

No. C553 *Andrea Doria*

Late in the 'fifties, the Italians were able to buy the Terrier from America to fill their SAM requirements. A pair of ships were designed and ordered but, in the time required to build them, valuable experience on the system was gained by the conversion in 1960 of the obsolescent cruiser *Garibaldi* for use as a trials ship.

Thus, when the two *Dorias* were completed in 1964, they could take advantage of ready-trained crews. The contrast between the older cruiser and the newcomers is a very interesting comment on the changes in 'cruiser thinking' over the elapsed thirty-odd years. *Garibaldi* was of the long, slim form associated with the high speed which was *de rigeur* with Italian cruisers. The *Dorias* were a product of international thinking, still possessing much individuality but beamier and slower, designed to deploy not only the Terrier but also a flight of four Agusta-Bell 240B AS helicopters.

They are a handsome pair of ships, with their tonnage putting them in the same bracket as the British County class. Their superstructure is much higher and square which gives them a more 'big-ship' appearance than the British ships with their destroyer-like profile.

Flush decked, their forecastle deck runs back in a graceful sheerline, flattening into the helicopter deck aft. This area is about 100 feet in length, the hull below flaring out from a flattish run to give a rectangular shape to it. A large door provides access into the hangar in the after end of the superstructure, which is high and boxy to accommodate it. This contrasts with the later *Veneto,* which has a lift to strike helicopters below for stowage. A penalty for the superstructure

hangar is paid in the intrusion of the uptakes which lead to the after funnel above. The forward funnel is integral with the bridge structure and almost undetectable except for the sloping funnel cap.

Before either funnel is a clean, unstayed pole mast. Each bears a fair selection of arrays and looks prone to vibrate. The radars are American and of earlier vintage than those in the *Veneto.* There is an SPS 39 on the mainmast to supply the Terriers and SPS12 long range search antenna on the fore. The positions of these are reversed on the later ship.

The twin Terrier launcher is in 'A' position with the two associated SPG 55 directors unusually far apart, one on the bridge top and the other in 'B' position. American practice will be to replace their Terrier missiles by the new Standard MR, but it is not known if these will be carried by the Italian ships.

Secondary, surface armament is vested in eight automatic DP 3-inch guns. These are in single mountings, four forward around the bridge structure and the rest at the upper corners of the hangar, on tower supports to give them better arcs of fire.

The helicopters are the main AS weapon of the ship, using AS torpedoes on information received from their own dunking sonars or from the hull-mounted set which the *Dorias* need to be self-supporting. Six AS torpedo tubes can also be carried aboard ship.

Although the Harrier S/VTOL fighter has operated successfully from the *Doria's* flightdeck, the ship is really too small to deploy them operationally.

de Zeven Provincien Cruiser (Guided Missile)   Netherlands

Units: No. C802 *de Zeven Provincien* (ex-*de Ruyter*, ex-*Eendracht*, ex-*Kijkduin*)
Laid Down: 1939
Launched: 1950
Completed: 1953
Displacement: 9,500 standard
11,900 Deep Load
Length (o.a.): 615ft
Beam: 57ft
Draught: 22ft
Machinery: Geared steam turbines 2 shafts
85,000shp for 32 knots
Armament: One—Twin SAM launcher
Four—6-inch (2 × 2)
Six—57mm (3 × 2)
Four—40mm (4 × 1)
For others of same class, see:
Almirante Grau (Peru)

This vessel is one of a pair of cruisers with somewhat chequered careers, not the least puzzling part of which concerned their names. Laid down in 1939 in different Rotterdam shipyards they were originally named *Kijkduin* and *de Zeven Provincien*. The former for some reason was then renamed *Eendracht* and, later, *de Ruyter*. Neither ship had

been launched when, in May 1940, the Netherlands were occupied. The more advanced hull of *de Ruyter* was slowly progressed under German supervision and launched in 1944—as *de Zeven Provincien*. Presumably this name, rather than that of the national hero, was more acceptable to the Germans and the fact that a Dutch name was retained at all may have been a gesture in the hope that a new Dutch Navy would eventually operated alongside the Reichsmarine. She was nowhere near complete at the war's end and was summarily re-christened *de Ruyter* by the Dutch.

Work on the real *de Zeven Provincien* was then recommenced, but postwar austerities kept construction down to such a slow pace that she was not launched until 1950.

Early impressions gave a conventional profile, but when they were completed in 1953, each sported a curious forefunnel/mast combination as used earlier on the British *Daring* and *Weapon* classes and later repeated by the Dutch on the *Friesland* and *Holland* groups.

The braced tripod mainmast was originally sited abaft the after funnel. Detrimental effects of stack gases on antennae caused it to be shifted on both ships to a situation where its legs were around the funnel casing.

In 1958, plans were announced to update the ships by the addition of guided missiles. Only de Zeven Provincien, the newer ship, was to be taken in hand to start with and she was reconstructed in 1962-4.

Among external changes, the mainmast was again moved to the more conventional site abaft the after funnel but increased in height to give the American SPS 39 antenna adequate clearance. The forecastle deck, which originally ran aft as far as X-turret, was continued right aft, making the ship flush-decked and much heavier in appearance.

Both after turrets of the main battery were removed together, with the twin 57mm turret which superfired them. In 'Y' position was mounted a twin Terrier missile launcher, loaded through a low wedge-shaped structure immediately forward of it.

Forward of this again are the two tiered Terrier directors.

The prime function of the 20-mile ranged missiles is defence against low flying aircraft, although they are of a rather early type. They are still supported by six 57mm guns and four 6-inch which, with automatic laying and operation and an elevation of 60° are fully dual-purpose.

The overall appearance of the ship is now reminiscent of the American cruiser conversions and the difficulties of building a 'production-line' missile system into a fine-lined and closely sub-divided hull was underlined by the fact that de Ruyter was never similarly converted and has since been sold to Peru (q.v.). de Zeven Provincien was updated in 1971 and is scheduled to last for about another two years.

Tromp Guided Missile Frigate

Netherlands

Units: No. F801 Tromp
No. F806 de Ruyter

	Tromp	de Ruyter
Laid Down:	1971	1971
Launched:	1973	1974
Completed:	1975	1976

Displacement: 3,400 standard
5,400 Deep Load
Length (o.a.): 453ft
Beam: 49ft
Draught: 15ft
Machinery: Two Olympus gas turbines 44,000shp total
Two cruise type gas turbines 8,000shp total
2 shafts for 28 knots
Armament: Two—Twin Exocet SSM launchers (possibly)
One—Twin Tartar SAM launcher
One—Sea Sparrow BPDMS launcher
Two—120mm (4.7-inch) guns (1 × 2)

The enormous advantage in hitting power of the guided missile when compared with the conventional gun results in a smaller ship to perform the same functions as its predecessor. A fine example of this is the class of two frigates the Dutch now have under construction. Bearers of the honoured names of Tromp and de Ruyter, they are scheduled for completion in 1975/6 and are specifically designed as replacements for the two de Ruyter class cruisers, of which the name ship has already been sold to Peru.

Referred to by the Dutch as 'large frigates', they are appreciably larger than the British Type 42 'destroyers', demonstrating once again the limitations of nomenclature.

They are not dissimilar in profile to the Type 42's but have no immediate counterpart in the RN, the best comparison for size being the Russian Kashin's.

As is normal with the omnifunctional warship of

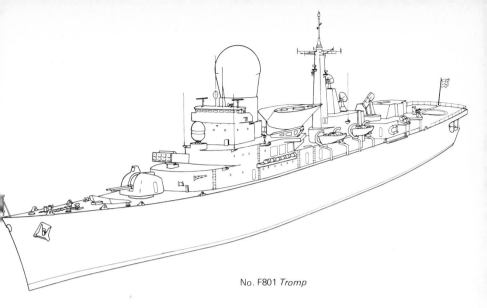

No. F801 *Tromp*

today the design is complex and expensive, with the 453-foot hull housing up to three separate missile systems, guns, a helicopter and the necessary mass of electronics for search and guidance.

Some of the 'cubic' for this inventory has been gained by the adoption of all-gas turbine propulsion. The two controllable pitch propellers are each driven by a 27,000shp Rolls Royce Olympus derated to 22,000shp for an extended life. Maximum speed is about 28 knots but fuel economy and extended range are achieved by the addition of two smaller Rolls Royce Tyne gas turbines of about 4,000shp each which can be clutched into the main gearboxes and used for normal cruising. In this mode they will run efficiently at optimum speed with the Olympus units shut down. The uptakes are veed out conspicuously in a variation on the Russian pattern in order to carry the highly corrosive hot exhaust gases clear of the ship's after structure.

The main AA armament is the twin Terrier mount aft. As the US Navy is planning to replace this missile with the Standard MR, now entering service, it is possible that these will eventually be carried, with a similar range of about 10 miles. Surveillance is by a Hollandse Signaal Apparaten 3-D set whose antenna is housed within the conspicuous radome above the bridge.

Short range backup is given by the BPDMS Seasparrow mounted in 'B' position. This is controlled by the fire control in the adjacent smaller radome, which also lays the fire of the twin 100mm automatic gun turret. As an economy measure, this mounting was refitted for further use after its removal from the discarded destroyer *Gelderland*.

Early drawings show a pair of Exocet-type SSM launchers on either side between funnel and bridge but it is not clear if these will finally be fitted. A WG 13 helicopter in a hangar aft confers the AS ability of the class.

As is becoming common with smaller classes, both vessels were built in a covered facility.

Babur Light Cruiser

Pakistan

Units: No. 84 *Babur* (ex-HMS *Diadem*)
Laid Down: 1939
Launched: 1942
Completed: 1944
Displacement: 5,900 standard
7,600 Deep Load
Length (o.a.): 512ft
Beam: 52ft
Draught: 18ft
Machinery: Geared steam turbines 4 shafts
62,000shp for 32 knots
Armament: Eight — 5.25-inch (4 × 2)
Fourteen — 40mm (5 × 2) + (4 × 1)
Six — 21-inch TT
There have been few classes of recent years more elegant than the first group of *Didos*. Dating from 1940-2 they were really purpose-built versions of the converted 'C' class ships of World War I. Here, the original 6-inch armament was replaced by modern HA 4-inch weapons. They proved to be quite efficient AA ships but, unfortunately, their capacity for firing ammunition was better than their capacity for carrying it.

To improve firepower in this new AA cruiser, the calibre chosen was 5.25-inch, using standard twin mountings as incorporated in the *King George V* class and, later, *Vanguard*. The hull was of sufficient size to deploy five of these mountings and the unusual layout of three super-firing turrets was adopted forward.

37

The function of this type was close-support for a task force or convoy, a duty which they performed superlatively well in the Mediterranean in particular (an excellent example being under Vian's resolute handling at the second battle of Sirte) and belying their rather fragile appearance. They were lean, low ships with the appearance of overgrown destroyers, the rake of the funnels and masts complementing the long gun barrels.

Before the first group of eleven was complete war had begun and a second group of five was commenced. Known as the 'Modified Dido' class, its ships varied from their predecessors primarily in the suppression of the high-mounted 'Q' turret. This was due both to need to reduce topweight and to a shortage of mountings—each new battleship requiring eight.

As with the *Colony* class, the masts and funnels on the new group 'went vertical' giving them a rather cut-down aspect. Protection was improved but still on a very light scale of 3-inch maximum on side belts and 2-inches on turrets.

Spartan of this group was lost off Anzio and, of the surviving four, two went to New Zealand. *Diadem* of the remaining pair was sold to Pakistan

in 1956, arriving in her new country the following year after an extended refit. She undertook duties as flagship after being renamed *Babur*.

As the Pakistan Navy operates a mixed bag of World War II vintage ex-British destroyers, *Babur*'s role is somewhat akin to that of the Light Cruiser 'Destroyer Leaders' of World War I.

Having more accommodation than other units of the Pakistan Navy, she was modified in 1961 to double as a training ship for cadets.

The class was never fitted with aircraft and catapult and the handling crane, so conspicuous in other classes, is also lacking. Surprisingly the two triple torpedo tube banks, sided at the after funnel, have been retained. Indeed the ship has been changed in appearance remarkably little since her construction and is still very typically a World War II cruiser.

Fire control and search radars are now very much outdated but can be handled by the limited technological backup available. The single calibre main armament (compare with combined 6-inch and 4-inch on other British classes) simplify requirements for directors and associated equipment.

Almirante Grau Cruiser — Peru

Units: No. 81 *Almirante Grau* (ex-HMNS *de Ruyter*)
Laid Down: 1939
Launched: 1944
Completed: 1953
Displacement: 9,500 standard
11,900 Deep Load
Length (o.a.): 615ft
Beam: 57ft
Draught: 22ft
Machinery: Geared steam turbines 2 shafts 85,000shp for 32 knots
Armament: Eight—6-inch guns (4 × 2)
Eight—57mm AA guns (4 × 2)
Eight—40mm AA guns (8 × 1)
For others of same class, see:
de Zeven Provincien (Netherlands)

One of a pair laid down at Rotterdam within months of each other during 1939, this ship suffered the fate of her sister when the Netherlands were occupied in 1940. For a while work ceased on both hulls, but was resumed at slow time under German supervision. This unit was launched in 1944 as the *de Zeven Provincien* but the other hull was still on the stocks when the war ended. As neither had been badly damaged, work began again on them at a slow rate. The launched hull was renamed *de Ruyter* by the Dutch and the other, not launched until 1950, took the name of *de Zeven Provincien* in turn.

Early drawings show no difference in the final armament layout but the profile had a more attractive and better proportioned appearance with two short, tapered funnels and straightforward tripod masts. The rapid wartime developments in radar and communications had, however, resulted in a proliferation of antennae which were virtually standard fittings by the time that work was resumed in 1946 and later drawings show heavier masts with cross-bracing and higher funnels. This complexity in top-hamper was further aggravated by new developments in the further seven years that it took to complete the ships and substantial support was required for the eventual mix of American and Dutch-built arrays, which were dominated by the enormous antenna of the Philips LWO search set.

Corrosion problems with stack gases obviously caused concern as several combinations have been tried of masts and funnels, ending in a rather unlovely arrangement where the masts were made of substantial height and constructed around and part of the funnel casing, the forefunnel particularly being an early example of a 'mack'.

Armament layout exemplifies the Dutch love of symmetry. Long barrelled Bofors-type 6-inch guns are housed in four twin turrets. Eight 57mm weapons are also twinned, with turrets on the centreline superfiring 'B' and 'X' positions and the other two sided in the waist. Eight 40mm guns are mounted singly along the superstructure sides—four forward and four aft.

All major guns are fully automatic and radar-laid. They have a dual-purpose role with the 6-inch being capable of a 60° elevation.

The two cruisers gave the necessary fire-power to form a balanced task group in conjunction with the single Dutch carrier *Karel Doorman*. This latter ship, however, was prematurely sold to Argentina in 1968 following fire damage, leaving the cruisers without a real function.

The newer ship, *de Zeven Provincien,* had been converted by 1964 to deploy the American Terrier missile. As with most conversions of this nature, the resulting less-than-perfect compromise was bought at higher cost than planned. *de Ruyter* was never converted and it was only a matter of time before she was sold out of the increasingly missile-dominated waters of Europe. In 1972, she hoisted the Peruvian flag where her 57mm guns introduced a new calibre and complicated an already sizable logistics problem.

On transfer, she was involved in yet more exchange of name, as she took that of the ex-HMS *Newfoundland* which in turn, was renamed *Capitan Quiñones.*

No. 83 *Capitan Quiñones* (ex-No. 81 *Almirante Grau*)

Bolognesi Cruiser   Peru

Units: No. 82 *Coronel Bolognesi* (ex-HMS *Ceylon*)
No. 83 *Capitan Quiñones* (ex-*Almirante Grau,* ex-
HMS *Newfoundland*)

	Bolognesi	*Quiñones*
Laid Down:	1939	1939
Launched:	1942	1941
Completed:	1943	1942

Displacement: 8,800 standard
11,100 Deep Load
Length (o.a.): 555ft
Beam: 64ft
Draught: 20ft
Machinery: Geared steam turbines 4 shafts
72,000shp for 31 knots
Armament: Nine—6-inch guns (3 × 3)
Eight—4-inch guns DP (4 × 2)
Twelve/Eighteen—40mm AA guns
For others of the same class, see:
Mysore (India)

At the close of World War II, Peru had a
small-ship navy. Far removed from combat zones,
she had also refrained from entering into the
rivalries of the South American ABC fleets
(Argentine, Brazil and Chile). Not surprisingly,
therefore, there was room for modernisation as the
fleet's most powerful units were a pair of elegant
but obsolete Vickers-built cruisers some 40 years
old.

Signs of the old competition for fire-power began
to show among the South American fleets in the
later 'forties and were solved neatly by the US Navy
transferring superfluous warships equally, so as to
give overall advantage to none of them. The
heaviest units involved in these transfers were
half a dozen large light cruisers of the *Brooklyn/St.
Louis* class and one of these, *St. Louis* herself,
was, at one time, earmarked for sale to Peru, but
this transaction never materialised and the ship
became one of a pair that hoisted the Brazilian flag.

Peru then acquired—rather more usefully—
several smaller flotilla vessels, although she still felt
the need for larger ships to patrol her exposed and
not inconsiderable coastline. Consequently in
1959/60 the later Colony-class cruisers
Newfoundland and *Ceylon* were purchased from
the Royal Navy.

They belonged to a trio (*Uganda* was the third)
which were a modified version of the eight *Fijis*
which immediately preceded them. In an effort to
reduce topweight, their triple 6-inch X turret was
suppressed from the outset in favour of an
additional twin 4-inch HA mounting and additional
smaller weapons were fitted. This sub-class was
among the first of the RN cruisers to be up-dated in
the 'fifties. In the course of modernisation they lost
their sided triple torpedo tubes and the X-position
4-inch mounting made way in its turn for extra
40mm weapons. Improvements in search and
director radars were to the detriment of their earlier
austere good looks; to support the weight of the
extra antennae, both ships had their foremasts
replaced by unsightly lattice masts stepped hard
against the forefunnel. *Newfoundland* (now
Quiñones) gained a light lattice mainmast in
addition, which now gives a recognition feature
different from her sister, who still preserves the
original tripod mainmast.

No. 82 *Coronel Bolognesi*

The former vessel has also the 'glasshouse' destroyer-style HA directors, sided by the foremast. *Ceylon* (now *Bolognesi*) has a fully enclosed bridge with two levels of windows all around the bridge front.

Except for the plating-in of the torpedo-tube aperture for the provision of extra accommodation, the ships have changed little in appearance since their transfer.

Quiñones bore the name *Almirante Grau* and the pennant number '81' until 1973, when both were transferred to the newly acquired ex-Dutch cruiser *de Ruyter*. This latter ship, incidentally, provides an interesting difference in national designs in that she disposes some 85,000shp on only two shafts whilst the ex-RN ships have 72,000shp on four.

These large ships are very greedy on crew by modern standards (their combined manpower would be sufficient to man twelve of the Mk 10 frigates building for Brazil) and their advancing years must make them due for replacement quite shortly.

Dedalo Aircraft Carrier   Spain

Units: No. PHO1 *Dedalo* (ex-USS *Cabot* AVT 3, ex-CVL28, ex-*Wilmington* CL79)
Laid Down: 1942
Launched: 1943
Completed: 1943
Displacement: 11,000 standard
15,800 Deep Load
Length (o.a.): 623ft
Beam: 71.5ft
Draught: 26ft
Machinery: Geared steam turbines 4 shafts
100,000shp for 32 knots
Armament: Twenty-six—40mm (2 × 4) +
(9 × 2)
Aircraft: About 20 helicopters

None of the great sea powers had fully realised during the build up to World War II what a vital part seaborne air power would play. This situation was remedied by the Americans with extreme thoroughness through a crash programme of Escort Carriers known variously as 'Woolworth Carriers' or 'Baby

Flat-tops'. The earliest were converted merchantment but a similar-sized series of purpose-built ships was also commenced. Although their 19 knots were adequate for convoy or AS duties they were insufficent for use with a task group.

Thus, nine hulls of Cleveland-class cruisers were converted to small carriers with a useful speed of 32 knots. Building up these fine hull forms presented many problems close akin to those faced during earlier conversions such as the *Furious* and *Lexington* classes. Besides stability problems was the question of including uptakes from boiler rooms spread over a considerable length of hull. Extensive trunking was avoided by employing a characteristic row of four stumpy funnels.

Reduction of topweight to a minimum resulted in an unarmoured flight deck.

Avgas mains running along the underside resulted in a great potential hazard which the loss of the *Princeton* at Leyte Gulf showed only too well.

Two further units of the class, *Cabot* and *Bataan*,

were converted in the 'fifties into specialist AS ships, being termed 'Hunter-killer Carriers'.

The previously large capacity of 40 aircraft was reduced to 20 plus. As these were much heavier than earlier aircraft, the flight deck and hangar deck were both strengthened and a catapult installed. Magazine layouts were changed, new electronics installed and two funnels were removed as part of stability correction.

The original heavy armament of four 5-inch guns was never fitted, only light automatic weapons being included. These now number about 26 × 40mm.

The pair were re-classified from CVL to AVT and put back into reserve with their still unconverted sisters. *Cabot* remained thus until 1967 when she was reactivated and transferred to the Spanish Navy for five years on loan. Renamed *Dédalo,* she was purchased outright at the end of the loan period.

Now 33 years old she is the only one of her type left in service but still supplies the Spanish Navy with useful AS capacity. Although an aircraft carrier she has been operating almost exclusively as a helicopter carrier, with a mixed bag of about 20 Sikorsky and Agusta-Bells.

A new dimension has recently been added, by successful sea trials of the Harrier on board *Dédalo*. These are wanted by the Spaniards but the UK Government will not supply them for political reasons. Eight have, therefore, been ordered from the US for delivery in late 1975 with options held for about 20 more.

Practice in the operational use of these will be gained on *Dédalo* which presumably will have to soldier on until 1979, when the Spaniards hope to commission their first home-built carrier, *Almirante Carrero*.

This ship will be a close copy of the proposed American Sea Control ships and may well be the first ship to deploy the Harrier in a purpose-built capacity.

Galicia Landing Ship Dock

Spain

Units: No. TA31 *Galicia* (ex-USS *San Marcos,* LSD25)
Laid Down: 1944
Launched: 1945
Completed: 1945
Displacement: 4,800 standard
9,400 Deep Load
Length (o.a.): 458ft
Beam: 72ft
Draught: 18ft
Machinery: Geared steam turbines 2 shafts
7,000shp for 15 knots
Armament: Twelve—40mm (2 × 4) + (2 × 2)
Capacity: 18 LCM or
3 LCU or
32 LVT
For others of same class, see:
Nafkratoussa (Greece)

In proportion to the size of the Spanish fleet, the tonnage of the Amphibious Warfare element is quite large. The reason lies in the interests that Spain still has in numerous islands and enclaves on the African continent. These are largely undeveloped and wanting in deep water harbours and facilities so that emergency help or military intervention must, of necessity be 'over the beach'.

It was, nevertheless, not until the 'sixties that Spain began collecting tonnage, largely from American sources. She gained experience on LSM's and LCT's which were later supplemented by a couple of Amphibious Transports (an ex-Victory class APA and an ex-C2 type AKA) each of which can lift about 24 small LCA's using ship's gear. This type of handling has limitations, however, particularly in open roadsteads subject to heavy swells, the normal conditions on the African coast.

In 1971-2, therefore, a needed reinforcement was made with the acquisition of three ex-American County-class LST's and, more significantly, an LSD. She was the *San Marcos* (LSD25) of the Cabildo class and was renamed *Galicia.*

This class of LSD dates from the end of World War II and consists of ships small by later standards. They are still very useful, however, for limited size operations. The dock area extends forward under the superstructure with the low-profile engines and boilers beneath, exhausting through sided uptakes which do not impinge on loading space. This area is tailored around various mixes of minor landing craft, usually either 3 LCU's or 18 LCM's.

LCU's (Landing Craft, Utility) fall into three main groups which vary between 105 and 125 feet on the waterline. The largest type has a deadweight capacity of about 200 tons and can accommodate three M-103 or M-48 tanks. They are driven by four diesels coupled to twin shafts and have an excellent range of over 1,000 miles although their design—particularly forward—does not give them any great open sea capabilities.

LCM's (Landing Craft, Mechanised) are smaller craft of two main types, the LCM 6 and the LCM 8. The latter is the larger with a 60-ton capacity, large enough for an M-48 tank. The LCM 6 can carry up to 34 tons of mixed cargo.

The docking well is spanned just forward of the stern gate by a removable platform which can support a helicopter. This confers the ability to put a holding party ashore to cover a landing or to put stores, including light transport and artillery, at inaccessible points.

A large crane is on either beam abaft the funnels and can be used for reloading craft on return trips, greater flexibility being conferred by the use of pontoons which can be floated out and joined to form a jetty alongside.

Up to 500 troops with their equipment can be carried on short trips in rather sparse accommodation.

The armament now consists of 40mm weapons, the single 5-inch formerly mounted forward of the bridge having been removed.

Canarias Heavy Cruiser — Spain

Units: No. C21 *Canarias*
Laid Down: 1928
Launched: 1931
Completed: 1936
Displacement: 10,300 standard
13,300 Deep Load
Length (o.a.): 636ft
Beam: 64ft
Draught: 21ft
Machinery: Geared steam turbines 2 shafts
92,000shp for 32 knots
Armament: Eight—8-inch (4 × 2)
Eight—4.7-inch (8 × 1)
Five—40mm

The effects of the 1922 Washington Treaty left a stamp on the ships of all major naval powers. Limitations on cruisers included a maximum tonnage of 10,000 and gun calibre not exceeding 8-inch. Anxious not to be outdone by foreign units, naval architects often designed up to the limits rather than down. Much ingenuity was used in the necessary compromise that resulted, some countries going for maximum armament and some for maximum speed. Both of these were bought at the expense of protection.

Britain, still with her world-wide imperial commitments, needed cruisers of good range and habitability, backed by a reasonable armament and speed. The resultant *County* classes of 1926-9 combined all these requirements. The main armament was paired in four large, twin, power-operated turrets which absorbed much of the permissible displacement. Further inroads were made by the large engines of 80,000shp necessary for a sea-speed in excess of 32 knots.

Capacity was vital for long range missions and it was decided virtually to dispense with armour.

The weight thus saved was worked into the vast hull, whose massive freeboard, crowned by three raked funnels presented an appearance best described as majestic, certainly unique. Their imposing aspect commanded admiration from abroad, notably from Spain who obtained licence from Britain to build a pair of modified versions in her own yards. Warships have always been long a-building in Spain, but even allowing for the depressed state of the world's economy, these were especially protracted. Laid down in 1928, *Baleares* and *Canarias* were not completed until 1936.

In appearance, hulls and turrets were closely akin

to the *Countys*, but the rest suffered from a bad dose of the 'Odeon architecture', so common at this time. The bridge structure, without a foremast, resembled a castle keep but paled beside the incredible funnel, an arched trunked affair with slab sides and enormous proportions. The secondary armament was increased in calibre from 4-inch to 4.7-inch and disposed in eight, single open mountings. An interesting feature were the four triple torpedo tube mountings; these were fixed above-water and firing on the beam through apertures in the shell plating just below the after superstructure.

A major simplification on the British design was the provision of only two shafts even though the power was considerably higher at 92,000shp.

Baleares had a short career, being a victim of the Civil War and *Canarias* performed duties as flagship of a neutral navy during World War II.

After a major refit of 1952-3, she emerged with the two capped funnels and a foremast which had been part of the original design. They greatly improved her appearance.

1960 saw removal of the redundant torpedo tubes and improved search and control radars required the mainmast to become a tripod.

Canarias was laid up at the end of 1974, releasing trained personnel for the newer flotilla vessels joining the fleet. It is doubtful if she will see more active service.

Ark Royal Aircraft Carrier

United Kingdom

Units: No. R09 *Ark Royal* (ex-*Irresistible*)
Laid Down: 1943
Launched: 1950
Completed: 1955
Displacement: 43,000 standard
Length (o.a.): 845ft
Beam: 113ft
Draught: 35ft
Width: 166ft (over flight deck)
Machinery: Geared steam turbines 4 shafts 152,000shp for 31 knots
Armament: Four—quadruple *Seacat* launchers to be fitted)
Aircraft: About 30 + 6 helicopters
Disposal: *Eagle* (1972)
Cancelled: *Africa*
  Eagle
  Gibraltar
  Malta } enlarged type
  New Zealand

As the monster animals of pre-history found themselves too large and vulnerable to exist in a changing world, so the great warship is dying in all but the two largest fleets and even these might find survival difficult in a modern full-scale war. Thus, *Ark Royal*, fourth bearer of an honoured name, finds herself the last Royal Navy unit of a long line that could impress by size alone.

She is survivor of a class of four that was born in the early days of World War II, when Britain's strange collection of fleet carriers was already showing deficiencies. Treaty limits forgotten, the new ships were to displace about 37,000 tons. Under war conditions, however, design and construction effort had to be devoted to those projects yielding highest return in the short term and smaller vessels took priority. This resulted in none of the class being launched before the end of the war.

Irresistible and *Audacious* were to have been the names of the first two, but these were changed to *Ark Royal* and *Eagle* as the names became available. The last pair and a projected enlarged trio of *Gibraltars* were cancelled.

Eagle, the furthest advanced, was launched in

1946 and almost completed before *Ark Royal* went into the water in 1950.

The 'Ark', when completed in 1955, was far larger than originally envisaged and arrived late enough to incorporate a 5 ½ ° angled deck and the first steam catapults. She also had an American-style deck-edge elevator to serve the upper hangar.

Armour, which had saved carriers many times from destruction by air attack, was on a generous scale, with a 4-inch flight deck over the hangar and the hangar deck itself some 2 ½ inches thick. A side belt of 4 ½ inches was also fitted.

Superstructure was slab-sided, clean and much larger than in previous British carriers.

With improvements in carrier design, each successive refit saw modifications. 'Traditional' British carrier armament had been sixteen 4.5-inch guns in eight twin DP turrets, two at 'each corner'. The two portside forward mounts were sacrificed early, being plated over to terminate the angled deck and removed in 1956. The complementary pair went in 1959 and the forward unit of each of the quarter pairs in 1964. Five years later the remaining two were landed. Guns were supposed to be replaced by four quadruple Seacat launchers, but these have yet to be fitted. She has, however, received a specialised 'Corvus' launcher for ECM Chaff — thus, even if she *can't* shoot at anything she *can* hide from it!

The side elevator intruded on hangar space and was largely redundant by virtue of the angled deck; it was, therefore, removed in 1959. Improved guidance systems and more powerful catapults were fitted in 1961.

Built in the era of small strike aircraft, she needed updating by 1967. After a three-year refit, she came out with a fully angled deck and the ability to operate up to 30 Phantom and Buccaneer aircraft (compared with her original 100) and a flight of Wessex helicopters. New masts bearing long-range antennae have greatly changed her profile.

With changing policies and a pending cut back in the Fleet establishment, her future is very much in doubt.

Bulwark Helicopter Carrier

Units: No. R08 *Bulwark*
Laid Down: 1945
Launched: 1948
Completed: 1954
Converted: 1959-60
Displacement: 23,300 standard
Length (o.a.): 738ft
Beam: 90ft
Draught: 28ft
Machinery: Geared steam turbines 2 shafts
76,000shp for 28 knots
Armament: Two—sextuple rocket projectors
40mm AA (number varies)
Helicopters: About 20 Wessex
Disposal: *Albion* (1972)
Centaur (1971)
Cancelled: *Arrogant*
Monmouth
Polyphemus
Hermes

It was realised, even during the course of their construction, that the light Fleet Carriers would have limitations—essentially they would be too slow and too small to operate as front line carriers but yet too complex and too expensive to rival the simple expendability of the utility escort carriers. A class of eight 'stretched' versions was therefore projected. The close of hostilities resulted in the cancellation of four of these and the remaining quartet—known as the *Hermes* class—joined the postwar log-jam of incomplete British carriers.

Unlike many of the 'Light Fleets', none of the larger class was completed only to 'go foreign'. Construction was recommenced in the late 'forties at a leisurely pace, with *Albion*, *Bulwark* and *Centaur* completing in 1953-4 and *Hermes* being held back, becoming a ship different enough to be treated as a separate class.

Some 40 feet longer than their predecessors, the *Centaurs* as they were known were little shorter than the 'I'-class carriers that were the backbone of RN air power in the later 'forties. They were some 9,000 tons greater in displacement than the *Majestics* and a modest increase in speed of only 4 knots demanded almost twice the engine power. They were fitted from the outset with an 'interim' angled deck of 5½° and a pair of hydraulic catapults, although the latter were exchanged in *Centaur* for steam catapults in 1957.

The changing role of the Royal Navy was amply demonstrated when the *Bulwark*, barely five years after first commissioning, was taken in hand for conversion into what became known popularly as a 'Commando Carrier'.

In truth, modern strike aircraft had been so rapidly increasing in size that this class was really too small to handle them, little in the way of modification being able to compensate for lack of hangar and deck space.

The 'treatment' now consisted primarily of removing all fixed-wing aircraft equipment, such as catapults, arrestor gear and landing aids and remarking the flight deck for nine helicopter pads. Some 20 Wessex and Army-type Sioux helicopters are now carried, the latter being used primarily in a reconnaissance role after a landing.

About 750 troops can be accommodated but the greater part of their transport has to be carried on the flight deck as the hangar has little spare capacity. Four LCVP's (Landing Craft, Vehicle Personnel) are carried aft, two on either side under special heavy-duty davits. These craft with the helicopters can speedily put ashore a Commando force with light vehicles and artillery. This type of force is typically used in a holding operation and the ship carries enough stores to keep it supplied until it is withdrawn on relief by more powerful forces. The inability of this type of ship to put armour support 'over the beach' is a drawback, subsequently rectified in the purpose-built *Fearless* class.

The Wessex helicopters carried are versatile craft used not only for transport but also, after conversion aboard, able to deploy air-to-surface missiles either for shore support or against submarines.

Albion was similarly converted soon after *Bulwark*, but in spite of a larger troop capacity, was listed for disposal in 1972.

Centaur was never rebuilt and was disposed of in 1971.

1975 defence cut-backs have advanced the planned end of *Bulwark's* active life to 1976.

Hermes Helicopter Carrier

Units: No. R12 *Hermes*
Laid Down: 1944
Launched: 1953
Completed: 1959
Converted: 1971-3
Displacement: 23,900 standard
Length (o.a.): 744ft
Beam: 90ft
Draught: 29ft
Machinery: Geared steam turbines 2 shafts
76,000shp for 28 knots
Armament: Two—quadruple *Seacat* launchers
Helicopters: About 20, dependent upon type

Hermes began life as a fourth unit of the Centaur class, but was completed a considerable time after them and with so many differences that she was always treated as a one-ship class. Incomplete at the war's end, she occupied a building slip until 1952 when her builders brought her to launching state in order to use the slip for other work. Launched in 1953, she was laid up until 1957 when fitting-out began. She was eventually finished in 1959, showing a profile close akin to the rebuilt *Victorious*, featuring a strongly tapered lattice mast abaft the funnel which, itself, lacked the old-style Admiralty top.

The bridge was dominated by the enormous Type 984 radar, which resembled an out-sized searchlight. This set, which provided advanced presentation of incoming data in 3-D form, was designed to be the nerve-centre of a carrier task force, providing information for compatible ships to operate as a closely co-ordinated group.

But the day of the large conventional RN carrier was in its evening and only the two sets ever went to sea operationally.

After the CVA-01 project was axed, the escorts designed to complement this advanced technology were either re-designed or cancelled, the only survivor being *Bristol* (q.v.).

The angled deck on *Hermes* was overhung by the largest possible amount sufficient to fit a deck-edge lift. *Ark Royal* (q.v.) had had hers removed as it encroached on hangar space but this new pattern

was entirely external to the hull, being little more than part of the flight deck running on vertical guides with access to the hangar via a door in the shell plating.

Joining the fleet in 1960, *Hermes* was in every respect an up-to-date carrier but was still too small to operate more than a handful of modern large strike aircraft.

During the refit of 1964-6, she lost her conventional light AA armament of 40mm weapons and gained two quadruple *Seacat* SAM launchers. One of these, together with its director, is mounted on a sponson on either side, aft.

It was not surprising when she was taken in hand in 1971 for conversion into a 'commando carrier'. As with previous rebuildings of this nature, her external appearance was not changed drastically. The superfluous 984 was landed and replaced by a single-array Type 965 surveillance radar. A crane was added abaft the island for handling equipment to and from the four LCVP's which are slung in heavy duty davits, two to a side, aft.

Like *Bulwark,* she now operates only helicopters, a mixture of up to 20 Wessex and Sioux. She has, therefore, lost all fixed-wing aircraft fittings such as catapults, arrestor gear and landing aids. The angled deck has been retained, however, mainly because its removal would mean the loss of the second elevator. The deck has been marked differently for helicopter pads—only 8 compared with *Bulwark's* 9. She is to be refitted in 1976 to increase her AS potential. Both carriers could operate Harrier-type S/VTOL aircraft without difficulty, but their future is rather clouded by proposed cut-backs in Fleet strength, with replacement purpose-designed ships already suffering.

Fearless Landing Ship (Dock)   United Kingdom

No. L10 *Fearless*

Units: No. L10 *Fearless*
No. L11 *Intrepid*

	Fearless	Intrepid
Laid Down:	1962	1963
Launched:	1963	1964
Completed:	1965	1967

Displacement: 11,100 standard
Length (o.a.): 520ft
Beam: 80ft
Draught: 21ft (Ballasted 32ft max)
Machinery: Geared steam turbines 2 shafts 22,000shp for 21 knots
Armament: Four—quadruple *Seacat* launchers Two—40mm AA (2 × 1)
Helicopters: Six Wessex (no hangar space)

Towards the end of World War II the RN operated a few LSD's which had been transferred from the US Navy. The problems facing the RN in its normal spheres of interest are different from those undertaken by the US in the Pacific War but the comparative unsophistication of the units operated under the White Ensign was still sufficient to demonstrate their possible uses and their design was sound enough to dictate that of many subsequent classes.

Basically, the cheap LST can operate armour 'over the beach', but has limited range, seaworthiness and accommodation; complex conversions such as the *Bulwark* (q.v.) can land troops and light transport, but cannot follow up with heavy armour. There was clearly a case for a specialised design of ship that could land anything and yet operate with reasonable seakindliness (and alone if necessary).

The LSD was, therefore, modernised and built as

49

the two *Fearless* class which closely followed the pair of American *Raleighs,* not only in size but also in that their docking well is rather small in relation to overall length.

Layout is rather dominated by the double hulled construction, with the dock area separating the two sides and vehicle and general storage decks ahead. The machinery is of low profile and does not intrude on the spaces above, the uptakes being sided. Boiler and engine spaces are laid out en echelon, which accounts for the characteristic staggered funnel arrangement.

The ships are designed to accommodate up to 700 troops with their equipment, transport, armour and artillery. All this is placed ashore and maintained by four LCM (9)'s housed in the well and up to six Wessex helicopters which are operated from the deck which spans the docking well for the greater part of its length.

The LCM (9)'s were developed for this application and are twin-screwed diesel-propelled craft, 85 feet in length and capable of carrying two main battle tanks or 100 tons of mixed load. They act as ferries for transport which is stowed on two vehicle decks and the upper deck, all of which are interconnected by ramps. The mode of operation is standard, with the mother ship flooding down until the water levels inside and out are equalised, whereupon the large sterngate is lowered to provide free passage both in and out.

Four 43-foot LCVP's are carried in davits to transport personnel. They can carry 35 equipped troops or two light vehicles which would be loaded via the crane aft.

Either ship is expected to act independently if required and both have been equipped as headquarters ships. They have larger superstructures than their American equivalents, housing quite elaborate communications systems. Indeed, military personnel are carried to operate the shore communication network and to operate as beach parties in the event of a landing.

Both ships have operated satellite communication systems, being among the world's first to be so equipped.

Armament—mainly four quadruple *Seacat* launchers—is purely defensive, the ships operating under escort in heavily contested zones.

Defence cutbacks may take *Fearless* prematurely out of service in 1976.

Tiger Helicopter Cruiser

United Kingdom

Units: No. C99 *Blake* (ex-*Tiger*, ex-*Blake*)
No. C20 *Tiger* (ex-*Bellerophon*)

	Blake	Tiger
Laid Down:	1942	1941
Launched:	1945	1945
Completed:	1961	1959

Displacement: 9,950 standard
Length (o.a.): 567ft
Beam: 64ft

Draught: 22ft
Machinery: Geared steam turbines 4 shafts 80,000shp for 31 knots
Armament: Two—6-inch DP guns (1 × 2)
Two—3-inch DP guns (1 × 2)
Two—quadruple *Seacat* AA missile launchers
Helicopters: Four Seaking
Disposals: *Lion* (1974)
Hawke (BU 1946)

No. C20 *Tiger*

Few cruisers were actually ordered during World War II except a couple of groups of improved Crown Colonies. One group of ten projected units was commenced with the laying down of four, *Defence, Blake, Hawke* and *Tiger*. Of these, *Hawke* was never launched and *Tiger* had exchanged names with an enlarged version to be named *Bellerophon*. The other six were cancelled.

Three near-sisters of the *Minotaur* class were completed after the war but the structurally complete *Tigers* (or *Defences* as they were then known) were laid up for a very considerable period. This was because they were to carry a new automatic gun armament, the post-war development of which was rather lengthy.

It was not until 1954 that the go-ahead was given for completion, with *Defence* taking the name *Lion* in 1957. Completed in 1959-61, the trio looked at first sight to be orthodox British cruisers but the difference lay in their weapon fit.

Where nine 6-inch guns could have been expected in three triple turrets, there were only four of these weapons in two twin mountings in 'A' and 'Y' positions. These were new automatic guns with a rate of fire of about 20 rounds per minute or up to eight times that of the earlier manually operated weapons. The water jackets surrounding the barrels gave them the appearance of 8-inch guns, an impression enhanced by the large gunhouses. The size and weight of these atuomatic installations were good reasons for only two, with the added complication of rapid-feed ammunition paths.

The secondary armament was also new. In 'B' position and on either side abaft the after funnel was a twin 3-inch turret containing guns of a new (70 calibre) British pattern. These replaced the familiar eight 4-inch HA guns and had a rate of fire of almost 80 rounds per minute.

The *Tigers* were among the last conventional cruisers built and were obsolescent on completion with more advanced ship types coming forward. 1964 saw the introduction of the French *Jeanne d'Arc* (q.v.) and the Italian *Dorias* (q.v.) and these may well have influenced the next phase. *Blake*, only four years old, was taken in hand in 1965 for conversion into a Command Helicopter Cruiser, with *Tiger* following in 1968. In contrast to the foreign designs, however, the *Tigers* look strange indeed.

From the mainmast aft, the hull was raised two decks with a 130-foot flight deck on top. To achieve the necessary width for this from the slim after end of the cruiser hull, a considerable flare has been required. At the forward end of this deck is a vast box-like hangar for the four Seaking helicopters. This small complement is hardly good value for the very considerable sum spent on the conversion and was the probable reason for the disposal of *Lion,* without rebuilding, in 1972.

Harrier V/STOL aircraft have operated successfully from the flight deck although the real operational value of this is questionable in view of the small numbers that could be deployed. The four Seakings undoubtedly confer a real AS potential to the ship and the close range AA capabilities have been enhanced by the substitution of quadruple Sea Cat launchers for the waist 3-inch mountings.

Invincible Helicopter Cruiser

United Kingdom

Units: *Invincible*
Laid Down: 1973
Launched: 1976
Completed: 1979
Displacement: 20,000 standard
Length (o.a.): 650ft
Beam: 84ft
Draught: 25ft
Width: 100ft (across flight deck)
Machinery: Four—Olympus and Two—Tyne cruising gas turbines
4 shafts total 110,000shp for c.30 knots
Armament: One—quadruple Exocet SSM launcher
Two—twin Sea Dart SAM launchers
Aircraft: Up to 20 Seaking helicopter equivalents or 10 Seakings and 6 V/STOL *Sea Harrier* equivalents

The history of this ship has been dogged by changes in policy and it has been doubtful on several occasions whether she would ever be completed. Her raison d'etre stemmed primarily from the Government decision not to proceed with the CVA-01 Fleet Carrier project and to run down the Fleet Air Arm. It was successfully argued that some ship-borne air power was necessary if the RN was to remain a reckonable force and, as the term 'Aircraft Carrier' was politically unacceptable the rather ambiguous euphemism of 'Through-deck Cruiser' was adopted. She is nevertheless, a small carrier which has been updated to modern requirements. The nearest equivalents are the Russian *Kurils* (q.v.) and the proposed American SCS (q.v.). It will be interesting to see whether the simple, inexpensive design of the latter, together with its good capacity, does not make it better value although its design philosophy is slightly different.

Invincible features a long, narrow island superstructure offset to starboard but with an access path between it and the deck edge. The island is dominated by a pair of tapered funnels of unequal height and with the large dimensions demanded by gas turbine propulsion. They appear to be built on top of the main air-intake houses.

The flight deck has no apparent angle and has parking space on the starboard side before and aft of the island. This deck terminates 70 feet short of the bows, with a half-deck drop to the mercantile-type forecastle. The reason for this peculiarity is not clear although it does make the term 'cruiser' more acceptable aesthetically.

No guns are fitted but on the forecastle, offset to starboard, is mounted a quadruple Exocet SSM launcher. Adjacent, on the centre line, is a twin

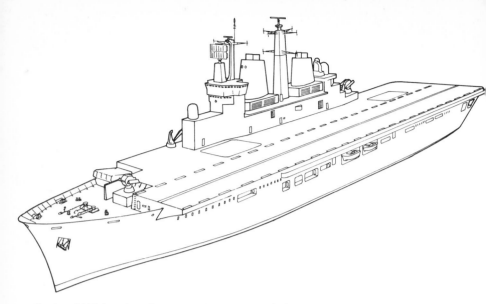

Seadart SAM launcher. A second of these is scheduled to be fitted but its position is not yet known with certainty. The Seadarts are controlled through the Type 909 radars which are housed under the conspicuous domes on the island.

Other radars include the double 965 whose massive array sits atop the bridge and the new standard 992 at the mainmast head.

Gas turbine propulsion in this size of warship is novel although experience has been gained with similar sized merchant ships. The ship can cruise economically with the two small Tynes on two shafts but this speed can be boosted rapidly by four Olympus gas turbines. The high initial cost of this arrangement is offset by its compactness and high availability and the ease with which it can be automated means a substantial reduction in engine-room staff.

It is not yet known what the final aircraft complement will be. The ship's dimensions suggest that she could carry about 15 Seaking helicopters. Preference would be for about half this number together with a section of V/STOL aircraft such as the Sea Harrier.

This aircraft can greatly increase its range and/or payload if given a short take off run and for this the through deck makes sense. Besides its strike potential, the Harrier has also been found to be an excellent vehicle for the rapid sonobuoy marking of submarines, giving the slower follow-up helicopters a better chance of a kill. No arrestor gear or catapults are fitted.

If the ship is successful, Iran may order one and the RN could get two more.

County Guided Missile Destroyer   United Kingdom

Units: No. D18 *Antrim*
No. D02 *Devonshire*
No. D20 *Fife*
No. D19 *Glamorgan*

No. D06 *Hampshire*
No. D12 *Kent*
No. D16 *London*
No. D21 *Norfolk*

	Antrim	Devonshire	Fife	Glamorgan	Hampshire	Kent	London	Norfolk
Laid Down:	1966	1959	1962	1962	1959	1960	1960	1966
Launched:	1967	1960	1964	1964	1961	1961	1961	1967
Completed:	1970	1962	1966	1966	1963	1963	1963	1970

Displacement: 5,450 standard
Length (o.a.): 520.5ft
Beam: 54ft
Draught: 20ft
Machinery: Geared steam turbines of 30,000shp
Four G6 gas turbines of 30,000shp
Total 60,000 for 32 knots. 2 shafts
Armament: One—twin Seaslug SAM launcher

One—quadruple Exocet SSM launcher in *Antrim, Fife, Glamorgan* and *Norfolk*
Four—4.5-inch DP guns (2 × 2) in *Devonshire, Hampshire, Kent* and *London*
Two—4.5-inch DP guns (1 × 2) in *Antrim, Fife, Glamorgan* and *Norfolk*
Helicopter: One Wessex

These handsome ships demonstrate a problem consequent upon designing a ship and its weapon system concurrently; the weapon system invariably turns out to be bulkier than the original estimates resulting in many re-castings of the ships' design, with inevitable delays. The *Countys* were planned to be of about 4,000 tons; they emerged at 5,400 tons standard displacement.

Created as a vehicle for the RN's first missile, Seaslug, the class retained a gun armament powerful by modern standards and represent an interesting bridge between the old-style escort and the new.

The low super-destroyer appearance set a precedent for subsequent RN classes. In order to be able to 'shut-down' under nuclear fall-out, no scuttles were provided in the hull. This, paradoxically, contributed to the high standards of habitation aboard; to avoid a feeling of entombment, close attention had to be paid to air-conditioning and layout.

The class divides into two distinct groups, with *Devonshire*, *Hampshire*, *Kent* and *London* completed in 1962-3 and *Antrim*, *Fife*, *Glamorgan* and *Norfolk* in 1966-70. The most prominent external difference between the groups is the single Type 965 array on the older ships and a double unit on the newer.

Forward, the ships have a 'cruiser' layout with the superimposed 'B' turret on a higher level which is taken out to the sides of the ship. This level does not, however, drop again abaft the bridge but continues to within 50 feet of the stern, where it drops to a low quarterdeck. Here is mounted the rather cumbersome twin launcher of the Seaslug.

The Mk 1 Seaslug was effective only against aircraft but the Mk 2 in the later ships has a limited effectiveness against surface targets, together with a better performance against the low-flying, radar-dodging aircraft. Best range is about 25 miles

and it could be retro-fitted to the earlier ships. Direction is from the Type 901 radar, looking like a large searchlight at the after end of the superstructure.

Short-range protection against aircraft is provided by both the 4.5-inch DP guns forward and the two quadruple Seacat missile launchers which, with their directors, are grouped around the after funnel.

AS potential relys entirely upon the Wessex helicopter carried abaft the superstructure at a high level above the Seaslug magazine.

A new development commenced in 1974 when *Norfolk* became the first to mount a quadruple Exocet SSM in place of 'B' turret.

The rest of the later quartet are also to be modified similarly. Exocet is a 20-mile weapon, very low flying and difficult to jam with ECM. (Initially guided by the ship, the missile homes actively in the final flight phase.) There is no room for magazine or handling arrangements, so no reloads are carried in peacetime. Thus, three separate guided weapon systems are incorporated.

Propulsion is by COSAG, with a steam turbine and two gas turbines on either shaft. Although the latter are not the marinised aircraft engines used in later classes, they were useful in proving the advantages of their type, compactness, immediate power from cold and ease of automatic control.

Defence cutbacks have put *Devonshire* on the disposal list (1975) with *Hampshire* to join her in 1976. The future of *Kent* and *London* must also be regarded with doubts.

Bristol Guided Missile Destroyer

United Kingdom

Units: No. D23 *Bristol*
Laid Down: 1967
Launched: 1969
Completed: 1973
Displacement: 5,650 standard
Length (o.a.): 507ft
Beam: 55ft
Draught: 21ft
Machinery: Geared steam turbines of 30,000shp
Two Olympus gas turbines of 44,000shp
Total: 74,000shp for 30 knots. 2 shafts
Armament: One — twin Seadart AA launcher
One — Ikara AS launcher
One — Mk 10 triple barrelled Limbo AS mortar
One — 4.5-inch DP gun

This, the first three-funneller to join the RN since the *Manxmans,* is a 'one-off', the only survivor of the projected Type 82 Class and an echo of naval thinking of the early 'sixties. Aircraft carriers were then still the acknowledged capital ships but, although they were powerful units in themselves, they still needed escorting against threats that they were not specifically designed to counter. Besides the obvious submarine menace, a new threat had developed from a single aircraft armed with a stand-off bomb of considerable range or the small, missile-armed FPB.

The Type 82's were designed as vehicles for the new Seadart missile and to complement the early warning system on the carrier being screened. Seadart is a more compact successor to the Seaslug carried by the *County* class with a range of about 20 miles against the earlier weapon's 25. Its

shorter overall length, however, allows it to be stowed vertically ('coke-bottle' stowage) and the twin launcher aft accepts them thus; the system is therefore much less cumbersome than the Seaslug's and more rounds can be carried.

Seadart is primarily an AA missile but it has a fast reaction time and can intercept incoming missiles in flight, employing semi-active homing with the target 'illuminated' by the Type 909 radars sited beneath the prominent domes. This versatile missile has also a limited capacity against surface targets. No close-range Seacat missiles need to be carried as in earlier ships.

Bristol is also only the second ship in the RN to carry the Australian designed Ikara missile. A measure of the faith placed in this weapon is that no helicopter is normally shipped, although a pad is provided right aft. The launcher is situated forward in the zareba abaft the 4.5-inch gun. Like the American ASROC or the French Malafon, it carries a homing torpedo to the vicinity of its target before dropping it. Close-range backup for this expensive weapon lies in the standard Limbo three-barrelled AS mortar in a well, aft.

The single, 4.5-inch gun is housed in the new Vickers Mk 8 turret. Fully automatic and un-manned, it is also directed by the 909 radar.

COSAG propulsion is provided, with the steam turbine set reinforced by two Olympus gas turbines. These can be run at the same time as the steam plant to give a rapid speed boost or alone to give immediate getaway. For normal cruising, the longer-life steam turbines are used alone. These exhaust through the forward funnel with the gas

turbines exhausting through the paired after funnels. These latter are unique, with most other designs favouring vee-form uptakes housed in either a single large funnel or a 'mack'.

In addition to the 909 radars, *Bristol* has a double 965 long range surveillance antenna on the foremast and the new Type 992 general purpose set on the tall main mast.

She proved a most expensive ship to build although her highly automated systems will save money on manpower in the long run. In losing one role she has gained another. Not only does she act as trials ship for the new weapons systems but she is also a prestige shop-window in an age where 'showing the flag' is still important, not least to promote the important export trade in arms.

Nimitz Aircraft Carrier United States

Units: No. CVAN 68 *Chester W. Nimitz*
No. CVAN 69 *Dwight D. Eisenhower*
No. CVN 70 *Carl Vinson*

	C. W. Nimitz	D. D. Eisenhower	C. Vinson
Laid Down:	1968	1970	1975
Launched:	1972	1974	1979
Completed:	1975	1976	1981

Displacement: 78,000 standard
91,500 Deep Load
Length (o.a.): 1,092ft
Beam: 134ft
Draught: 38ft
Width: 252ft (over flight deck)
Machinery: Two nuclear reactors
Geared steam turbines 4 shafts
280,000shp for c.33 knots
Armament: Three — BPDMS (Sea Sparrow) launchers
Aircraft: 90

The US Navy is still firmly wedded to the concept of the large fleet carrier but the complexity and size of

modern aircraft have escalated its dimensions and cost to a point of re-appraisal and this class must really be regarded as the ultimate. As at least one of the class is expected to cost over one thousand million dollars, future CV replacements will almost certainly be smaller. This trend could well be accelerated if the V/STOL aircraft is developed further.

Another point militating against such attractive targets is that they can have their every move monitored and hostilities could find them individually targetted from fixed shore sites.

The well-proven *Enterprise* (q.v.) has been used as the basis for the new design, which is slightly smaller but marginally heavier. In profile, however,

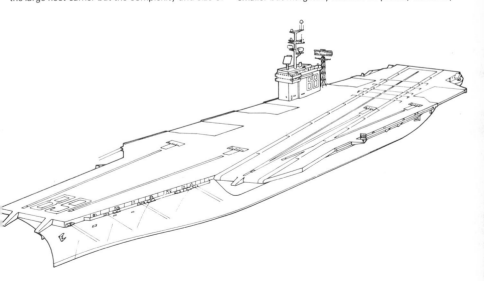

No. CVAN 68 *Chester W. Nimitz*

Nimitz is closer to the *Kitty Hawks* (q.v.), with the island well aft, two side elevators being forward of it and one aft.

As the stack on the 'conventionals' is very much built into the superstructure, its absence on this nuclear trio is not immediately obvious. One effect has been to resite the pole mast symmetrically on the island, i.e. farther aft. The lattice mast abaft the island carries the SPS-43 search antenna that was carried over the bridge in the earlier class. The square SPS-48 antenna familiar on GM frigates is mounted in this position for 3-D search. After the 'billboard' approach to antennae in the *Enterprise,* it is interesting to see the reversion to rotating aerials, suggesting limitations in the earlier arrangement.

As with earlier classes, the flight deck is asymmetric in plan, heavily sponsoned and with sufficient overhang to accommodate the deck-edge elevators entirely outboard of the hull, where they will not encroach on hangar space. Four steam catapults are fitted, two firing over the bows and two forward over the port sponson.

The first two of the trio are classified CVAN (attack carriers) but the third is a CVN (aircraft carrier) with the first two probably being modified later to this configuration. The reason for this stems from the smaller number of carriers deployed; each must be more versatile in order to undertake a greater variety of missions. Thus, as the specialist AS carriers are phased out, more AS aircraft will be shipped by what were previously attack carriers. This is not just a matter of changing aircraft as complex support facilities need to be re-arranged in turn. Sonar is not due to be fitted to the *Nimitz* class so AS data will have to be supplied from her own helicopters or escort ships.

The very comprehensive radar fit will permit close co-ordination with other ships of a task group but the present lack of suitable nuclear-propelled escorts will mean that these carriers cannot realise their full potential. Theoretically, they can steam indefinitely at high speed but they will be inhibited by their escorts' refuelling needs.

Advances in nuclear engineering have resulted in only two reactors being necessary per ship, compared with the eight in *Enterprise.* Experience in the latter has enabled the prediction to be made that the initial cores on the *Nimitz* will last some 12 years on normal steaming.

The size and complexity of ships such as these has resulted in fewer shipyards capable of building and servicing them. All nuclear carriers are now built in the one facility at Newport News, which could lead to problems in the event of war.

Enterprise Aircraft Carrier

United States

Units: No. CVAN 65 *Enterprise*
Laid Down: 1958
Launched: 1960
Completed: 1961
Displacement: 75,700 standard
89,600 Deep Load
Length (o.a.): 1,123ft
Beam: 113ft
Draught: 36ft
Width: 257ft (over flight deck)
Machinery: 8 A2W Westinghouse pressurised
water cooled reactors
Geared steam turbines 4 shafts
280,000shp for 33 knots max
Armament: Two — Basic Point Defense Missile
(Sea Sparrow) systems
Aircraft: 80-90

The 'Big' E's reign as the world's largèst warship lasted about 13 years until the commissioning of *Nimitz.* She was a result of the imaginative programme of the late 'fifties, when the feasibility of nuclear propulsion was investigated in several classes of ship, resulting also in the cruiser *Long Beach* (CGN 9) and the frigate *Bainbridge* (DLGN 25) in quick succession.

Like the other ships, *Enterprise* was very much a prototype and her total of eight reactors is large by today's standards, but she has given the experience of operation and confidence necessary to proceed with the *Nimitz* class. A slightly enlarged *Kitty Hawk,* she would have had a running mate in *Kennedy* had not the cost proved excessive.

The priority placed on her construction resulted in a building time similar to the conventional *Kitty Hawks,* and a vindication of the time and effort involved was the successful world circumnavigation by the whole nuclear squadron, when a distance of over 30,000 miles was covered — without refuelling.

The first set of reactor cores lasted for 3 years, with the ship steaming over 200,000 miles. *Enterprise* then returned to her builders at Newport News for an overhaul and refuel which lasted about eight months. This second fuel charge gave a 300,000-mile endurance over some 4 years, at only one-third the cost of the first. During the long refit of 1969-71, her builders effected a third recoring which has lasted to date. Another is shortly due and it is confidently expected that she will run for a further decade without attention. It is plain from these figures that the earlier caution has now been replaced by confident acceptance of the new system.

Deck layout is closely similar to that on the *Kitty Hawks* with the island again sited farther aft than usual, causing the characteristic 'bob-tailed' profile. This island is unique, being square in plan; a tower occupying a minimum of deck space. Its small dimensions are possible due to the lack of conventional funnel and uptakes.

Lack of corrosive stack gases allowed further experimentation with the 'bill-boarding' of radar antennae. These are here fixed arrays set behind the featureless rectangular panels on the sides of the island, an arrangement tried out at the same time in the *Long Beach.* Greater range and a lower incidence of mechanical failure were claimed for the

HMS *Bristol* lying at anchor in the Firth of Forth.
Robin Adshead

Sikorsky SH-3 Sea King of the 'Pacific Fleet Angels' of HC-1 passing USS *Midway.*   *Peter Kilduff*

A Hawker Siddeley Buccaneer Mk 2 of 809 Sqn Royal Navy being catapulted from HMS *Ark Royal*. More Buccaneers and Phantoms are on the flight deck. *Robin Adshead*

No. CVAN 65 *Enterprise*

arrangement but it was not included in the *Nimitz* class, so one must assume some limitations. The vertical panel screens the SPS-33 target tracking radar and the horizontal the SPS-32 range and bearing radars.

The island bears also the rotating arrays of search and navigation radars and is topped-off by a strange truncated conical structure bearing rings of ECM antennae.

Rather strangely, the *Enterprise* was completed without armament. This was an economy measure rather like the proverbial 'ha'porth of tar' and she was eventually retro-fitted with BPDMS Sea Sparrow launchers. Unlike *Kennedy* she has only two, both on sponsons aft.

Enterprise is not equipped with hull sonar and is still rated an attack carrier (CVAN). She will probably be eventually regraded CVN and carry a larger range of aircraft and ordnance. Lack of uptakes from the machinery spaces will give extra space and ease the inclusion of these extra facilities.

Kitty Hawk Aircraft Carrier

United States

Units: No. CV 63 *Kitty Hawk*
No. CVA 64 *Constellation*
No. CVA 66 *America*
No. CVA 67 *John F. Kennedy*

	Kitty Hawk	Constellation	America	John F. Kennedy
Laid Down:	1956	1957	1961	1964
Launched:	1960	1960	1964	1967
Completed:	1961	1961	1965	1968
Length (o.a.):	1,063ft	1,073ft	1,048ft	1,048ft
Beam:	130ft	130ft	130ft	130ft
Draught:	36ft	36ft	36ft	36ft
Flight deck width (max):	249ft	249ft	249ft	252ft

Displacement: 60,200 standard
80,800 Deep Load
(*JFK* 61,000 standard 87,000 Deep Load)
Machinery: Geared steam turbines 4 shafts
280,000shp for 33 knots max
Armament: Two — twin Terrier SAM launchers
(*JFK:* Three — Basic Point Defense Missile BPDMS
Sea Sparrow systems)
Aircraft: *Kitty Hawk* and *Constellation:* 70-80
America and *John F. Kennedy:* 80-90

This quartet is substantially similar to the earlier *Forrestals,* their construction time scales overlapping. *Kennedy,* the last of the group was originally to have been nuclear propelled (CVAN) but the cost of the installation was at that time insupportable and she reverted to CVA; the time taken over replanning was such that she was completed considerably later than her class-mates and incorporated enough modifications to be considered officially as a separate one-ship class.

The major external differences from the *Forrestals* stem from the modified flight deck layout. Both classes have this deck heavily sponsored for maximum area and each has four deck-edge elevators completely outboard of the hull, three to starboard and one to port.

In the *Forrestals,* two of the starboard-side elevators are abaft the island but the *Kitty Hawks* have two forward. This results in the island being positioned rather farther aft and this, coupled with the extra lattice mast abaft it, is the major recognition difference.

All the class are completely missile-armed, *Kitty Hawk* being the first thus in the US Navy. She, *Constellation* and *America* each have two twin Terrier SAM launchers. These are situated on boat-shaped sponsons on either quarter and associated with the SPS-30 search radar whose dish is on the lattice mast above the island. Actual control is by the directors adjacent to the launcher with target 'illumination' from another atop the bridge. An interesting feature is that the port launcher fires the RIM-2D beam-rider and the starboard the RIM-2F semi-active version of the Terrier. Allocation of a relevant missile will depend upon a target's range, height and speed, which information is fed from the rectangular SPS-52 3-D antennae into the ship's NTDS (Naval Tactical Data Systems).

By the time that *Kennedy* was completed, the trend was towards shorter-ranged missiles and shortly after completion she was fitted with three BPDMS Sea Sparrow launchers. These are fitted on either quarter and on the starboard bow, and fire a smaller missile with a range of only 7-10 miles. It is presumed that the distant threat can be dealt with by aircraft or by the escort with only the short-range targets to be taken seriously. This system demands an SPS-48 antenna on the second mast, a useful recognition point. *Kennedy* differs from the rest of the class also in being the only one with the funnel canted outboard to improve the clear flow for stack-gases; this feature is not immediately apparent in profile.

All four ships have an SPS-43 search antenna atop the bridge, farther forward than in the *Forrestals.* It is interesting that the two latest ships of the class, *America* and *Kennedy* are equipped with bow sonar domes, betrayed externally by the stem anchors, so mounted as to fall clear.

This fitting is in keeping with the philosophy of

No. CVA 67 *John F. Kennedy*

converting more attack carriers (CVA) to straight aircraft carriers (CV) and it can be expected that all four of the class will eventually be so designated and operating a wider variety of aircraft with, particularly, an enhanced AS capability.

Four steam catapults are fitted, two firing over the bows and two serving the angled deck to port.

Besides attack aircraft the mix includes EKA-3B Skywarrior ECM aircraft and E-2B Hawkeyes for early warning.

The 'high-speed carrier' tradition has been maintained with a very high power output for about 33 knots.

Forrestal Aircraft Carrier

United States

Units: No. CVA 59 *Forrestal*
No. CV 60 *Saratoga*
No. CVA 61 *Ranger*
No. CV 62 *Independence*

	Forrestal	Saratoga	Ranger	Independence
Laid Down:	1952	1952	1954	1955
Launched:	1954	1955	1956	1958
Completed:	1955	1956	1957	1959
Length (o.a.):	1,039ft	1,039ft	1,039ft	1,047ft
Beam:	130ft	130ft	130ft	130ft
Draught:	37ft	37ft	37ft	37ft
Flight deck width (max):	252ft	252ft	260ft	252ft

Displacement: 59,800 standard
78,000 Deep Load
Machinery: Geared steam tubines 4 shafts
280,000shp for 33 knots
(*Forrestal* 260,000shp)
Armament: Four—5-inch DP (4 × 1)
(except *Forrestal,* with one Sea Sparrow BPDMS)
Aircraft: About 80

The large, fast carrier so dominated US Naval thinking in the Pacific war that it was scarcely surprising that each succeeding class increased dramatically in size. The *Midways* were too late to play a part in the war, so their number was limited to three and work begun on a new design, half as large again, which was laid down in 1949. This ship, named *United States* (CVA 58), was conceived at at time when there was much rethinking on carrier design, particularly in the UK. Postwar financial restrictions proved fatal and the project was cancelled. The design was modified to include new

advances and, three years later, the keel of a lead ship for a projected class of six was laid. Named *Forrestal,* she was, far and away, the biggest carrier since the lone Japanese giant, *Shinano* (65,000 tons, 1944).

The new ships incorporated protected flight decks and enclosed 'hurricane bows' which removed two design weaknesses common to previous American carriers. Additional refinements were no less than four of the then new steam catapults and an angled deck. From the beginning, the Americans were more adventurous with the latter than the British, sponsoring the flight deck boldly on both sides with the width over the deck being twice the ship's beam. Four deck edge elevators were sited, outboard of the hull plating, with no centreline units. One of the elevators is sited, rather curiously, at the outboard end of the flight path, an aberration cured in later classes by moving it farther aft down the port side.

The island is compact and rectangular in profile,

similar to later classes, but is in a more orthodox position farther forward. The funnel is integral with this structure and shows only as a short, wide extension above it.

The class originally mounted eight single 5-inch guns, two 'at each corner'. These required extensive sponsons, particularly at the fine forward end and it was possible to slam these structures when pitching heavily. To avoid structural damage, it was necessary to reduce speed and this inhibited operating efficiency. Starting with *Forrestal,* therefore, conventional armament is being removed and replaced by the BPDMS Sea Sparrow system. Three will eventually be put into each ship together with SPS 58 radar to direct them against low-flying targets.

The ships are electronically well up-to-date and feature beside the large search antennae of the SPS-43 radar a specialised Carrier Controlled Approach antenna housed within the dome at the after end of the island. They have also a Naval Tactical Data System (NTDS) to co-ordinate operations not only with aircraft but with other ships of a group.

Hull sonar is not fitted but, in view of the fact that these ships are being re-rated CV from CVA, it is not impossible that it could be incorporated as, with the new designation, the carriers will have new flexibility in attack particularly enhanced in an AS direction.

As it is, reliance must needs be placed in the sonars of escorts or helicopters. These are Sikorsky SH-3 Seakings with backup from Grumman S-2E Tracker aircraft.

Except for several serious fires — rather too common in US carriers — the *Forrestal* design has proved a sound base for the development of later classes, which are closely similar. Indeed, the last two of the designed sextet, the *Kitty Hawk* and *Constellation* became eventually the lead pair of a new class.

Midway Aircraft Carrier

Units: No. CVA 41 *Midway*
No. CVA 42 *Franklin D. Roosevelt*
No. CVA 43 *Coral Sea*

	Midway	Roosevelt	Coral Sea
Laid Down:	1943	1943	1944
Launched:	1945	1945	1946
Completed:	1945	1945	1947

Displacement: 51,000 standard
64,000 Deep Load
(*Coral Sea* 52,500 standard)
Length (o.a.): 979ft
Beam: 121ft
Draught: 35ft
Width: 238ft (over flight deck)
Machinery: Geared steam turbines 4 shafts
212,000shp for 33 knots
Armament: Four—5-inch DP in *F.D. Roosevelt*
Three—5-inch DP in *Midway* and *Coral Sea*
Aircraft: About 70
Cancelled: CV 44
CV 56 and
CV 57

The *Midway* class is the surviving trio of a projected class of six, the remainder of which were cancelled at the close of hostilities. They represented the limits of carrier technology achieved in World War II, being designed with the benefit of some operational experience from the *Essex* class, although they were laid down long before the completion of this extensive group and, individually, of nearly twice the tonnage.

With only 1½ inches of armour on the flight deck, the *Essex* class ships were quite thin-skinned, relying on the strength of the hangar deck for further protection. The *Princeton* at Leyte Gulf demonstrated that a carrier could be lost by a fire on the hangar deck following the piercing of the flight deck; equally well, the tough hides of such British carriers as *Illustrious* and *Formidable* had shown the way to survival following severe damage 'up top'.

These lessons were ploughed back into the *Midway* design and much of the extra tonnage of these ships is accounted for by the stout flight deck.

No advance is without its price, however, and all this extra weight so high in the ship required a rethink on stability problems. All US Navy ships had been built to a standard requirement that they be fine enough for transit of the Panama Canal lock systems, enabling swift interchange of force between the Atlantic and Pacific fleets. This rule became a casualty with the required beam of the new carrier and no class of carrier since has started with the remotest chance of conforming to it.

Midway completed just too late to see any active service and the *Coral Sea,* close on her heels, took the name *F.D. Roosevelt* on the president's death. The third ship assumed the name *Coral Sea* but was a further two years before commissioning. They were originally classified CV and then CVB. Currently, they are CVA and it is doubtful if they have enough flexibility left in them to undergo the final regrade back to CV.

None of the class has ever been in reserve but all have been periodically updated. The original armament reflected the curtain barrage techniques of the Pacific War in its eighteen 5-inch and nearly 200 smaller guns. The latter weapons were later landed in favour of up to forty 3-inch weapons. In keeping with modern ideas, practically all conventional ordnance has now been removed, although the ships are not missile armed. Ironically, *Midway* was the first carrier to launch a guided missile, when a Regulus I was fired in 1947.

When completed the ships could operate over 130 of the then current aircraft. The increase in size of strike aircraft has reduced this number by almost half and greatly changed the layout of the deck.

No. CVA 41 *Midway*

The two centreline elevators have gone in favour of two on the starboard deck edge, fore and aft of the island. The third original elevator, a deck edge type 'midships on the port side, was retained as part of the angled deck overhang, but has since been moved farther aft in *Midway* and *Coral Sea*.

From the recognition point of view, this class is the only type of US carrier to have a distinct funnel. Forward of this was a braced tripod mast, now replaced by a tapered pole with a thick base. The overall profile is low.

Electronics are well up-to-date, particularly on the newly modernised *Midway*, and include an NTDS.

Hancock Aircraft Carrier

United States

Units: No. CVS 11 *Intrepid*
No. CVT 16 *Lexington* (ex-*Cabot*)
No. CVA 19 *Hancock* (ex-*Ticonderoga*)

No. CVA 31 *Bon Homme Richard*
No. CVA 34 *Oriskany*
No. CVA 38 *Shangri-La*

	Intrepid	Lexington	Hancock	Bon Homme Richard	Oriskany	Shangri-La
Laid Down:	1941	1941	1943	1943	1944	1943
Launched:	1943	1942	1944	1944	1945	1944
Completed:	1943	1943	1944	1944	1950	1944
Displacement:						
standard	32,800	32,800	32,800	32,800	33,250	32,800
Deep Load	42,000	39,000	44,700	44,700	44,700	42,000
Length (o.a.):	895ft	895ft	895ft	895ft	895ft	895
Beam:	103ft	103ft	103ft	103ft	107ft	103
Draught:	31ft	31ft	31ft	31ft	31ft	31
Flight deck width (max):	192ft	192ft	192ft	192ft	195ft	192

Machinery: Geared steam turbines 4 shafts 150,000shp for 32 knots
Armament: Four—5-inch DP (4 × 1) (none in *Lexington*)
Aircraft: CVA configuration, above 70
CVS configuration, above 45

For disposal, see improved *Essex* class

This class is one of the two small groups of carriers that comprise the survivors of the once-numerous *Essex* class; the groups differ only in the degrees of modernisation that they have undergone. Current designations are split between CVA (attack carrier), CVS (AS carrier) and CVT (training carrier) but these are quite flexible, as evinced by rapid re-rating and deployment off Vietnam of

No. CVT 16 *Lexington*

Intrepid and *Shangri-La* as Light Attack Carriers.

This switching between AS and attack roles is rather more complex a matter than a simple exchange of aircraft and a fair measure of reconstruction may ensue. Weight and dimensions of the new aircraft will decide (or be decided by) elevator configurations. Various types of fuel may be required and these must be both stored and run by pipe to refuelling points. Maintenance and repair of modern airframes require a complex facility that needs a 're-tool' with a change of aircraft. A new range of weaponry will be embarked requiring modified magazine arrangements and re-organis-ation within the armourer's department. Certainly not least of the modifications involve the change of emphasis in the Combat Information Centre.

Most of these veterans underwent two major facelifts in the 'fifties, designed primarily to enhance aircraft handling, with the addition of angled decks, reinforcement of complete flight decks, steam catapults and improved landing and approach aids.

They were also subject to the so-called FRAM II modifications of the 'sixties which, besides updating electronics, improved the habitability of the ships and were designed to extend their active life by a further five years.

The original twelve 5-inch guns have now been reduced to only four, although *Lexington* in her training role has none. They are the only American carriers remaining with a centreline elevator, which has a pointed forward end to accommodate the extra length of modern aircraft. Two deck edge elevators are also fitted. These are unusual in that they stow vertically against the hull when not in use, hingeing upward from the 'down' position and obviating the need of side doors.

The attack versions operate a mixture of the A-7 Corsair and the older A-4 Skyhawk. Crusaders can be carried in either the F-8 fighter configuration or the RF-8G reconnaissance version. The heavy Skywarrior is shipped in the EK-A-3B variant, which combines ECM duties with a useful tanker facility for in-flight refuelling of other aircraft. Early warning is given by the E-1B Tracer whose range supplements the SPS-43 system on the ship. As helicopters are usually carried in addition, some idea of the average maintenance problem may be appreciated.

An odd member of the group is *Oriskany*. Laid up after launching, she was completed some three years after the rest of the class and incorporated modifications which change her data somewhat. Despite her increased tonnage she features an aluminium flight deck and was equipped with heavier arrestor gear than her sisters.

The rebuilt profile of the class resembles the French *Foch* class. These are much of a size but have a squarer superstructure and an enclosed quarterdeck.

It would be expected that the phasing-out of these units will be continued and that only a limited life is left.

Improved Essex Aircraft Carrier

United States

Units: No. CVS 12 *Hornet* (ex-*Kearsarge*)
No. CVS 20 *Bennington*

	Hornet	Bennington
Laid Down:	1942	1942
Launched:	1943	1944
Completed:	1943	1944

Displacement: 33,000 standard
40,600 Deep Load
Length (o.a.): 890ft
Beam: 102ft
Draught: 31ft
Width: 196ft (over flight deck)
Machinery: Geared steam turbines 4 shafts
150,000shp for 32 knots
Armament: Four—5-inch (4 × 1)
Aircraft: About 45 including about 20 helicopters
Disposals of Essex class:

No.	Name	Date
CVS 9	*Essex*	1973
CVS 10	*Yorktown*	1973
AVT 8	*Franklin* (ex-CVS 13)	1964
CVS 14	*Ticonderoga*	1974
CVS 14	*Randolph*	1973
AVT 9	*Bunker Hill* (ex-CVS 17)	1966
CVS 18	*Wasp*	1972
LPH 4	*Boxer* (ex-CVS 21)	1969
AVT 10	*Leyte* (ex-CVS 32)	1969
CVS 33	*Kearsarge*	1973
CVS 36	*Antietam*	1973
LPH 5	*Princeton* (ex-CVS 37)	1970
CVS 39	*Lake Champlain*	1969
AVT 12	*Tarawa* (ex-CVS 40)	1967
LPH 8	*Valley Forge* (ex-CVS 45)	1970
AVT 11	*Philippine Sea* (ex-CVS 47)	1969

The US Navy realised well before the event that airpower would be crucially important in any Pacific War. As their carrier strength was still low, a design for a standard series was prepared which finally resulted in the end in some 32 sisters being ordered. The first 11 were ordered in 1940 and 24 were eventually completed, 23 between December 1942 and November 1946 and the solitary *Oriskany* some three years later. Construction was confined to a minimum number of yards, enabling series production to be adopted. This resulted in some fast building times, the *Hornet* for instance being built in only 15 months, from laying-down to commissioning, the launching being at an advanced state of fitting out.

Although none of the class was lost during hostilities, battle experience was ploughed-back into the newer ships as they were built, resulting in differences in armament and hull sub-division.

The design followed, in broad terms, that of early converted ships in as much as it consisted of a hull topped off with a 3-inch armoured deck. This was

No. CVS 12 *Hornet*

the hangar deck level and the flight deck was mounted above on a structure non-continuous with the hull. This system, found also in Japanese practice, conferred certain advantages in that a high, over-stiff structure was avoided. Flight decks could flex through expansion joints and openings in the shell allowed the pre-strike warm up of aero-engines without exhaust fume problems.

Disposition of the twelve 5-inch guns was unusual. Four were in single, open mountings on portside sponsons. The remainder were in four standard twin Mk 42 gunhouses superimposed forward and aft of the island, from which commanding position they could, in theory, fire over large arcs. During subsequent refits, they have been reduced to only four weapons of the old 38-calibre type, now disposed roughly one 'at each corner'. Earlier extensive close range weaponry was exchanged for some twenty-eight 3-inch guns which have since been removed altogether. No missiles have been fitted, although several deployed the Regulus whilst it was operational.

The original profile included a square-topped funnel and a low tripod mast but reconstruction in the 'fifties resulted in a taller island with a new-style pole mast topping off a combination structure from which the funnel protruded at a steep angle. The effect is not unpleasing and the class has retained its nicely balanced profile.

Not all the class were updated to the extent even of angled decks during postwar refits. These saw service as AVT's (Auxiliary Aircraft Transports) or LPH (Amphibious Assault Ships—not to be confused with the current purpose-built *Iwo Jimas*).

Hornet and *Bennington* both have angled decks but have never been updated sufficiently to operate the heavy current front line aircraft. They are, therefore, rated CVS (AS carriers) and operate a mixture of SH-3 Seaking helicopters for attack and E-1 Tracer and S-2 Tracker aircraft for early warning and detection. These aircraft are getting obsolescent and are due for replacement but will probably last the remaining life of their carriers. On retirement of these specialist ships—which also have hull sonar—there is little likelihood of straight replacement. The present CVA-to-CV conversion programme is designed to compensate for their loss.

Long Beach Guided Missile Cruiser

United States

Units: No. CGN 9 (ex-CGN 160, ex-CLGN 160) *Long Beach*
Laid Down: 1957
Launched: 1959
Completed: 1961
Displacement: 14,200 standard
16,250 Deep Load
Length (o.a.): 72ft
Beam: 73ft
Draught: 30ft
Machinery: Two C1W pressurised water cooled reactors
Geared steam turbines 2 shafts
80,000shp for 33 knots
Armament: One—twin *Talos* SAM/SSM launcher
Two—twin Terrier SAM launchers
Two—5-inch DP guns (2 × 1)
One—8 tube ASROC AS launcher
Two—triple AS torpedo tubes
Helicopters: One carried. No hangar

Obviously funnel-less and dominated by the great square bridge structure, the profile of this vessel is unmistakeable. She was very much ahead of her time when completed as the world's first nuclear propelled surface warship and various changes in name, size and armament during her gestation indicate the uncertainty of her final exact role.

Designed originally to be of about the same size and armament as the later *Bainbridge* (q.v.), she was to carry the name *Brooklyn,* but several changes were made in her missile armament which effectively doubled her size. She was destined to deploy not only tactical Talos and Terrier systems but the strategic Regulus II. The latter was an enormous 60-foot SSM with a range with nuclear

warhead of nearly 1,000 miles. It was really a submarine weapon and too cumbersome to survive.

The *Long Beach,* as she was now known, was actually under construction on the missile's demise and it was decided to utilise the space in the ship for eight vertical tubes for the new Polaris missile.

Building costs had quadrupled, however, and economies forced the abandonment of the Polaris in favour of a second Terrier launcher.

Thus, the final, and eminently more practical, missile armament lay in twin Terrier launchers in both 'A' and 'B' positions and a twin Talos launcher at the forward end of the wide quarterdeck which does duty also as a helicopter landing pad.

Terriers are fast reaction SAM's with a range of about 20 miles. Their two pairs of acquisition and guidance directors are mounted abaft 'B' position and atop the bridge structure. This type of missile is now being phased out in favour of the new Standard MR, but no plans have been announced regarding replacement.

Talos is a beam-riding SAM with a slant horizon range out to nearly 70 miles. It can carry a tactical nuclear warhead and be used in a limited anti-surface role, equipped with a semi-active homing head.

Like her nuclear compatriot *Enterprise,* the *Long Beach* has a billboard fixed radar array. 'Scanfar' radars, designated the SPS 32 and 33, are mounted behind the 'slabs' on the bridge structure. They are high performance units giving ranges, bearings and tracking information. A conventional mast tops-off the bridge structure, carrying the rotating scanners of search and navigational radars, ECM equipment

65

and a TACAN pod. The ship also has sonar in a bow dome, supplying data for the 8-barrelled ASROC launcher amidships. This weapon can be backed up by two triple AS torpedo tube banks and the helicopter when carried.

As in the case of several all-missile ships, it was realised later that the armament was over-powerful for use against small or 'soft' targets which could be encountered. Two single 5-inch 38 calibre DP guns were therefore fitted. They are sided at the after end of the 'midships gap.

Fitted with two reactors (compared with eight in the contemporary *Enterprise*) she steamed nearly 170,000 miles over four years before requiring a refuel.

She is unlikely to be repeated as a design as the same offensive power can now be tailored into a smaller hull. Inevitably, however, successive classes are increasing in size.

Photograph of *Long Beach* appears on pages 4-5.

Albany Guided Missile Cruiser

United States

Units: No. CG10 (ex-CA123) *Albany*
No. CG11 (ex-CA136) *Chicago*
No. CG12 (ex-CA74) *Columbus*

	Albany	Chicago	Columbus
Laid Down:	1944	1943	1943
Launched:	1945	1944	1944
Completed:	1946	1945	1945
Converted:	1962	1964	1962

Displacement: 13,900 standard
18,900 Deep Load
Length (o.a.): 673ft
Beam: 70ft
Draught: 27ft
Machinery: Geared steam tubines 4 shafts
120,000shp for 31 knots
Armament: Two—twin Talos SAM/SSM launchers
Two—twin Tartar SAM launchers
Two—5-inch DP guns (2 × 1)
One—eight tube ASROC AS launchers
Two—triple AS torpedo tubes
Helicopter: One carried. No hangar.

To all intents and purposes identical since their conversions, *Chicago* and *Columbus* belonged originally to the *Baltimore* class (q.v.) and *Albany* to the *Oregon City* class (q.v.). The main differences between these classes lay in their superstructure, with hull and machinery very similar in layout. Original plans called for three pilot conversions to the *Oregon City* (CA122), *Fall River* (CA131) and *Chicago* (CA136), to be followed-up by the *Rochester* (CA124) and *Bremerton* (CA130). In the event, the first two had substitutes and the last pair of conversions never took place owing to the high cost involved and the increasing potency of smaller purpose-built ships.

All three conversions commenced in 1959 in different yards. Each ship was stripped to the bare hull and all conventional armament and ammunition spaces removed.

The low 'cruiser' profile disappeared in the reconstruction of the missile disposition and its height required the use of much light alloy to compensate.

Dating from the same period as the *Long Beach* construction, they, too, were at one time destined to deploy eight Polaris launchers but this requirement was cancelled before reconstruction commenced.

No. CG10 *Albany*

The new main armament is now built around no less than four twin missile launchers, two Talos and two Tartar. The former, with their directors, are placed forward and aft, and the latter flank the bridge structure. Tartar is a 10-mile ranged SAM and, in spite of its smaller size, only one-third as many rounds are carried as *Long Beach* does for her Terriers. This demonstrates the limits of conversions.

The blast effects of the Tartars dictate the plain configuration of the lower bridge and the distinctive gap between it and the Talos director group.

Disposition of major antennae varies from ship to ship, but each carries a SPS-43 3-D mattress on the aftermost of the two enormous 'macks' which dominate the ships. *Albany,* which has since been up-dated electronically, mounts an SPS-48 antenna on the foremast whilst the other pair each have two SPS 30 dishes of an older search set.

Each has a hull-mounted sonar set, governing the fire control system for an ASROC launcher amidships. More target information can be supplied by helicopter borne sonar but, although a space is provided aft for the helicopter's pad, there is no hangar. Additional anti-submarine power is contained in two triple banks of Mk 32 torpedo tubes which can be shipped.

As with the *Long Beach,* the wisdom of an armament composed entirely of high performance missiles was questioned and two 5-inch, 38 calibre guns with their directors were mounted high up, flanking the after 'mack'. The macks provide not only a casing for the uptakes and auxiliary exhausts but also a vibration-free tower for major electronics, with protection for their vital leads.

Without doubt, these are three very imposing ships, but the conversions can only be regarded as far less than ideal. The missiles are now rather dated and the *Columbus* has already been earmarked for disposal. The *Chicago,* also unmodernised, will probably soon follow.

Converted Cleveland Guided Missile Cruiser   United States

Units: No. CG4 (ex-CLG4, ex-CL92) *Little Rock*
No. CG5 (ex-CLG5, ex-CL91) *Oklahoma City*

No. CLG6 (ex-CL82) *Providence*
No. CLG7 (ex-CL66) *Springfield*

	Little Rock	Oklahoma City	Providence	Springfield
Laid Down:	1943	1942	1943	1943
Launched:	1944	1944	1944	1944
Completed:	1945	1944	1945	1944
Converted:	1960	1960	1959	1960

Displacement: 10,700 standard
15,200 Deep Load
Length (o.a.): 610ft
Beam: 66ft
Draught: 25ft
Machinery: Geared steam turbines 4 shafts

100,000shp for 31 knots
Armament: One — twin Talos SAM launcher
(CLG3, 4 & 5 only)
One — twin Terrier SAM launcher (CLG6, 7 & 8 only)

No. CG4 *Little Rock*

Six—6-inch guns (2 × 3) ⎫
Six—5-inch guns (3 × 2) ⎬ CLG3 & 8 only
Three—6-inch guns (1 × 3) ⎫
Two—5-inch guns (1 × 2) ⎬ CLG4-7 only
Helicopter: Basic facilities for one. No hangar
Disposals: *Topeka* (CLG8, ex-CL67) 1973
Galveston (CLG3, ex-CL93) 1974

The *Clevelands* were a group of no less than 39
light cruisers—comparable to the British *Belfast* in
both size and armament—laid down in an extended
programme between July 1940 and September
1944. Only four shipbuilding yards were involved,
economy and construction times both gaining by
production runs. A typical building time was 22
months, although *Pasadena* (CL65) was completed
in only 16. Nine hulls were converted during
construction to fast escort carriers of the
Independence class and three were cancelled.
None was sunk but almost the complete class
was decommissioned rapidly after World War II.
In the mid-fifties, thirteen were earmarked for
conversion into hybrid gun-missile cruisers. These
were the *Birmingham* (CL62), *Vincennes* (CL64),
Pasadena (CL65), *Springfield* (CL66), *Topeka*
(CL67), *Providence* (CL82), *Miami* (CL89), *Astoria*
(CL90), *Oklahoma City* (CL91), *Little Rock* (CL92),
Galveston (CL93), *Amsterdam* (CL101) and *Atlanta*
(CL104).
As with most conversions of this type the
narrow, sub-compartmented hull proved much
more expensive and difficult to rebuild than had
been anticipated and, in the event, only six
conversions were carried out. These have vari-
ations and are officially grouped into two distinct
classes. CLG3, CG4 and CG5 deploy the Talos
SAM/SSM and CLG6 and 7 the smaller Terrier
SAM, both classes having one twin launcher in the
'Y' position. Superstructures were heavily re-

modelled, although not completely rebuilt as in the
Albany class conversions, and all convention
armament was removed from the after end.
To complicate classification however, CLG4
inclusive were fitted-out as flagships. The extra
accommodation thus required resulted in the bridg
structure being much enlarged and built forward
reducing the forward gun armament.
CLG3, the only remaining 'non-flagship', retain
both the triple turrets in 'A' and 'B' position
together with a twin 5-inch superfiring 'B' turre
and two further twin 5-inch gunhouses flanking the
original bridge structure. The four flagships have
the larger bridge which is not only longer than the
original, but wider. They have, therefore, sacrifice
both sided 5-inch gunhouses and the triple 6-inch
from 'B' position. The site of the latter has bee
filled by the twin 5-inch mounting previously
mounted abaft it.
The Terrier-armed ships CLG6 and 7 can be
identified from their near sisters by their three large
lattice masts. In lieu of the third mast, the Talos
ships have prominent platforms atop the afte
superstructure, bearing an SPS-30 dish and the
second mast a more dominant structure hard up
against the after funnel.
The SPS 30 is on the second mast in the Terrier
ships and both groups have the large mattress o
the SPS 43 on the foremast. The cantec
rectangular antenna of an SPS 39 or 52 3-D set is
mounted on the aftermast in all ships.
The quarterdeck has been laid out as a helicopter
pad but the old aircraft hangar cannot be used as
accommodation. Any AS capabilities are vested
entirely in the helicopter as there is neither hul
sonar nor ASROC.
The disposal of CLG8 marked the beginning of
the end for this 30-year-old class, which cannot
have much life left.

Virginia Guided Missile Frigate

Units: No. CGN 38 *Virginia*
No. CGN 39 *Texas*
No. CGN 40 *Mississippi*
No. CGN 41 *Arkansas*
No. CGN 42 (approved)

	Virginia	*Texas*	*Mississippi*	*Arkansas*
Laid Down:	1972	1973	1974	1975
Launched:	1974	1975	1976	—
Completed:	1975	1976	1977	—

Displacement: 10,000 Deep Load
Length (o.a.): 585ft
Beam: 61ft
Draught: 29ft
Machinery: Two—D26 pressurised water-cooled
reactors
Geared steam turbines 2 shafts
c. 72,000shp for c. 31 knots
Armament: Two—twin Mk 26 Standard MR/
ASROC launchers
Two—5-inch (Mk 45) DP guns (2 × 1)
Two—triple Mk 32 AS torpedo tubes
Helicopters: Two carried. Housed below

The naming of the larger frigate classes after State
of the Union seems to have signalled finally the
passing of the 'big gun' navy. Traditionally,
State names were borne by battleships and cruiser
were named after major cities; the latter category
will now signify nuclear attack submarines. Bu
where the big-gun Goliaths have been finally
displaced by missile-armed Davids, the usurpers
have proved so complex and expensive that they, ir
turn, will probably make way for simpler and
cheaper substitutes. It has been estimated that the
proposed DLGN 41 will cost about £125,000,000
even at 1974 prices and, where it was planned to
have about 30 nuclear escorts, it now appears that
8 will be the maximum.
The *Virginias* are a direct derivative of the pair of
Californias and very similar in appearance. The later
ships, however, have a less cluttered appearance
forward of the bridge and the foremast has been
moved forward to a point almost exactly amidships,
with the gap between the masts correspondingly
wider.

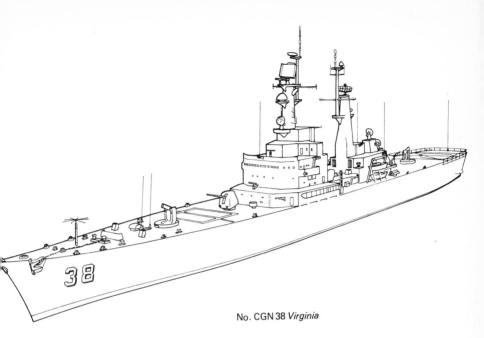

No. CGN 38 *Virginia*

A major difference, not immediately obvious, is that the hull is some eleven feet shorter, an advantage directly attributable to the lack of an ASROC launcher. This has been made possible by fitting two combination-type Tartar-D missile launchers. Again single units, they will fire both the Standard MR SAM and the ASROC through a complex mixed feed system from the magazine. The anti-air warfare (AAW) and anti-submarine warfare (ASW) fire control systems are more advanced than those of the *Californias* and designed for smooth interfacing, a vital need when common hardware, such as launchers, is used.

Two 5-inch lightweight gun mountings are again fitted, although the after one of the *Virginia's* is mounted one deck lower owing to the lack of the low deckhouse of the earlier design.

Another brief flirtation with fixed AS torpedo tubes has apparently had limitations for the two familiar tripled Mk 32 banks have reappeared, sided on the weather deck abreast the aft superstructure.

A new model sonar, the SQS-53, has been fitted. It is probably more compact in as much as the published draught for the class is rather less on a closely similar hull, suggesting a shallower bow dome.

Radars are similar to the earlier class, although both the SPS-48 and the SPS-40 are of later versions. The dome which probably contains the SPS-55 has been shifted to the leading side of the foremast. The rash of electronic counter-measure (ECM) pods which are so much a feature of Russian superstructures is noticeably absent on their American counterparts, whose slender topmasts betray little. More obvious are the 'chaff' rocket launchers placed at either end of the superstructure; the rockets from these scatter a complex array of false targets, designed to confuse incoming enemy missiles. Directors have been reduced in number and it would appear that both main launchers are controlled from the same pair.

Two helicopters are accommodated in the same manner as aboard the *Californias*. Machinery and reactors are also basically similar, although it is anticipated that refinements included will permit a steaming range of nearly three-quarters of a million miles before first refuelling.

California Guided Missile Frigate

United States

Units: No. CGN 36 *California*
No. CGN 37 *South Carolina*

	California	South Carolina
Laid Down:	1970	1970
Launched:	1971	1972
Completed:	1974	1974

Displacement: 10,200 Deep Load
Length (o.a.): 596ft
Beam: 61ft

Draught: 31ft
Machinery: Two—D26 pressurised water-cooled reactors
Geared steam turbines 2 shafts
c. 72,000shp for 31 knots
Armament: Two—single Tartar-D launchers for standard medium range (MR) SAM
Two—5-inch (Mk 45) DP guns (2 × 1)
One—8-tube ASROC launcher

No. CGN 36 *California*

Four—Mk 32 AS torpedo tubes
Helicopters: Two carried. Housed below

In the three-ship nuclear programme of the early 'sixties, there was a clear distinction in size between the cruiser *Long Beach* and the frigate *Bainbridge*. Those same processes of evolution that limited the former class to only one unit are now at work to increase the size of subsequent versions of the latter making type names meaningless. At over 10,000 tons, the *Californias* are equivalent in size to earlier heavy cruisers, although it could be argued from an historical standpoint that the term 'frigate' is more appropriate than 'cruiser' for this type of ship.

The increased size allows scope for a more versatile armament fit and it is interesting to compare with the next most recent class, the *Belknaps*.

The gun has a new importance; there are two 5-inch 54-calibre weapons in new single lightweight mountings, the second a direct replacement for the earlier 3-inch.

There are two missile launchers but each is a single mount of a new pattern termed the Tartar D. These have individual pairs of Mk 74 directors and are designed to fire the new standard MR missile, which is primarily an AA missile which has been given limited surface-to-surface capability pending the satisfactory introduction of the new Harpoon SSM into the fleet. As with other American frigates, no Point Defence Missile System is fitted and protection from an incoming enemy missile is largely from ECM.

The missile launchers do not handle ASROC and a separate 'pepperbox' launcher is sited directly forward of the bridge. It is reloadable through the small deckhouse adjacent. There is an updated version of the SQS-26 sonar for its control or data

from either of the two helicopters carried. Four fixed Mk 32 AS torpedo tubes are built into the ship, possibly firing wire-guided torpedoes through the aperture in the transom. These ships are designed primarily as a carrier group screen but are well able to operate independently. In this situation, AS effectiveness is greatly enhanced by the addition of a second helicopter.

The stowage of the helicopters has resulted in the reversion to the long, high freeboard characteristic of earlier cruisers, for the same reason— the hangar is below the quarterdeck. An elevator connects with the operations pad right aft.

Tophamper is neat and contrasts with the wilder eccentricities of some equivalent Russian classes. The two 'macks' are broadly similar to earlier versions and only the absence of exhaust ducts and black smoke bands betrays the fact that the ships are nuclear propelled. The general appearance brings to mind recent Italian designs.

Two reactors of similar type to the two prototype nuclear frigates are fitted, indicating the successful development of a standard power package. The ships are rather larger, however, and, unless there have been improvements in the heat exchangers, steam plant and hull form, they are likely to be marginally slower.

The radar fit includes the large rectangular antenna of the SPS-48 3-dimensional radar and an SPS-40 search radar on the mainmast. A new SPS-55 set is fitted, probably below the dome on the after side of the mainmast. An NTDS (Naval Tactical Data System) is linked to the various sensors, providing a high degree of control and co-ordination in action situations.

A third ship of the class, unnamed, was cancelled in favour of the new *Virginia* class (q.v.) whose notes also apply to a large degree.

Truxtun Guided Missile Frigate

United States

Units: No. CGN 35 *Truxtun*
Laid Down: 1963
Launched: 1964
Completed: 1967
Displacement: 8,200 standard
9,100 Deep Load
Length (o.a.): 564ft
Beam: 58ft
Draught: 31ft
Machinery: Two—D2G pressurised water-cooled reactors
Geared steam turbines 2 shafts
60,000shp for 31 knots
Armament: One—twin Terrier SAM/ASROC launcher
One—5-inch DP gun
Two—3-inch AA guns (2 × 1)
Four—fixed AS torpedo tubes (two Mk 32 and two Mk 25)
Helicopter: One

The *Belknap* (q.v.) class was planned to include ten conventionally powered frigates, but Congress insisted on one being nuclear propelled and the resultant ship, *Truxtun,* is really a stretched version with modified layout. At the time of the earlier three-ship nuclear programme, the gun was regarded as passé and only minimal conventional armament was fitted. It has since been recognised that there is still a place for modern gunnery and some retro-fitting has occurred. Thus *Truxtun,* laid down some four years after her near sister *Bainbridge,* shows a very different armament arrangement on a similar sized hull.

Conventional weaponry has been buttressed by a single 5-inch automatic DP gun forward. This is a 54-calibre weapon with a range out to 26,000 yards compared with the 17,000 yards of the older 38-calibre standard versions. There is an elevated deck abaft it in 'B' position, a strangely under-employed space at present occupied by only a couple of ECM chaff launchers.

Only one twin Terrier launcher is carried, mounted on the low quarterdeck which is slightly shorter than the *Bainbridge's.* Great space-saving efforts have been made compared with the earlier ship and this single launcher, a Model 7, is charged not only with firing either high or low level versions of the Terrier, but also ASROC missiles. The space saved in a comparatively small compass is considerable but bought at the expense of a complex rotating magazine designed to deliver on demand either of the 3,000lb SAM's or 1,000lb ASROC's. This is very much an 'all eggs in one basket' approach, and a fault in this system could rob the ship of her primary AA and AS capabilities.

One result of the economy of space is the provision of a helicopter pad elevated to weather deck level and forward of the launcher. This area is sheltered by the high after superstructure, which itself contains a hangar for a LAMPS helicopter. This is a complete weapon system in itself (described under Belknap class notes) and adds much to the ship's offensive power.

Between the two large and inelegant lattice masts and sided abreast the 'midships gap are two 3-inch DP guns mounted singly in open tubs. Below each of them is mounted a pair of Mk 32 AS torpedo tubes. These are built into the superstructure and fire over the beam. This unusual arrangement keeps everything under protective cover and is possible only because the torpedoes are 'homers' and do not need accurate laying. Two earlier pattern tubes are, in addition, built into the stern.

Truxtun has a near indentical power plant wit the earlier ship and a very similar hull which is slightly deeper draught and lacking the knuck forward. Radar systems are generally similar but later pattern and an NTDS has been fitted from th outset.

An interesting comment on the vagaries of sh naming is that this one is really spelled incorrectl The ship is named after Commodore Truxtc (1755-1822) who commanded with distinctic during the late 18th century war with France.

Bainbridge Guided Missile Frigate

United State

Units: No. CGN 25 *Bainbridge*
Laid Down: 1959
Launched: 1961
Completed: 1962
Displacement: 7,600 standard
8,600 Deep Load
Length (o.a.): 565ft
Beam: 58ft
Draught: 27ft
Machinery: Two—D2G pressurised water-cooled reactors
Geared steam turbines 2 shafts
60,000shp for 31 knots
Armament: Two—twin Terrier SAM launchers
Four—3-inch AA guns (2 × 2)
One—8-tube ASROC AS launcher
Two—triple Mk 32 AS torpedo tubes
Helicopter: One carried. No hangar

The third and smallest of the three-ship nuclear programme of the late 'fifties, *Bainbridge* is in some ways the most important. Warships sizes are decreasing and this 'one-off' showed the feasibility of nuclear propulsion in a hull no larger than that of a World War II AA cruiser. That her basic layout was good is reflected in the close similarity of later conventional frigates and the new nuclears now entering service.

The funnel-less profile is now less an obvious hallmark of the nuclear propelled frigate because of the popularity of the 'mack' combination in American designs, although *Bainbridge* has open lattice masts which betray the lack of uptakes within.

The low, fine-lined hull has a long knuckle forward and introduced a rather un-American feature in the drop in level aft to the quarterdeck. This feature did not last long, however, as the characteristic high freeboard has now been reintroduced in the *Californias* (q.v.) to accommodate a below-decks helicopter hangar.

Armament is AA and AS orientated with surface offensive power dependent upon two twin 3-inch gun mountings, disposed in open tubs on either side of the after superstructure.

There are two twin Terrier SAM launchers, one in 'A' position loading through a low ramped structure and the other on the lower quarterdeck loading through apertures in the hance. As with the installations on the *Kitty Hawk* class carriers, the

Terriers are of mixed type to cater for both high an low level targets. The associated pairs of director so much a part of American missile systems, a mounted prominently atop the bridge and lowe down aft.

Between the reload structure of the forwa Terrier mounting and the bridge front is an 8-tub non-reloadable ASROC pepperbox launcher. Th weapon is used in conjunction with the SQS-2 sonar, housed in a pronounced bulb at the forefoc This appendage, common to most mode American frigates, is betrayed externally by th bow, sharply raked to carry the stem-mounte anchor clear. The ASROC is an expensive weapo effective out to about 5 miles and closer-range threats are countered by Mk 32 homing torpedoe released from either of two triple banks of tubes. helicopter can be operated from the quarterdec pad to augment both attack and detection bu there are no hangar facilities, making it impossibl to regard the helicopter as a normal part of th ship's armament.

Prominent radars are the SPS-52, with i rectangular antenna on the foremast givin 3-dimensional information to the launch compute and the SPS-37 search set on the low mainmas These may well be changed in the course of current updating refit, known as an AAW c Anti-Air Warfare conversion. On its completior *Bainbridge* will be able to operate the Standard M missile and improvements in fire control will give faster reaction time. She will also have an NTD (Naval Tactical Data System), giving a better actio plot and the ability to co-ordinate closely wit similarly fitted units. *Bainbridge*, with her unlimite range, is very much a task force escort rather than general purpose frigate.

Leahy Guided Missile Frigate

United States

Units: No. CG 16 *Leahy*
No. CG 17 *Harry E. Yarnell*
No. CG18 *Worden*
No. CG 19 *Dale*
No. CG 20 *Richmond K. Turner*

No. CG 21 *Gridley*
No. CG 22 *England*
No. CG 23 *Halsey*
No. CG 24 *Reeves*

	Leahy	Yarnell	Worden	Dale	Turner	Gridley	England	Halsey	Reeves
Laid Down:	1959	1960	1960	1960	1961	1960	1960	1960	1960
Launched:	1961	1961	1961	1962	1963	1961	1962	1962	1962
Completed:	1962	1963	1963	1963	1964	1963	1963	1963	1964

Displacement: 5,700 standard
7,800 Deep Load
Length (o.a.): 547ft
Beam: 55ft
Draught: 25ft
Machinery: Geared steam turbines 2 shafts
85,000shp for 33 knots
Armament: Two—twin Terrier SAM launchers
Four—3-inch AA guns (2 × 2)
One—8 tube ASROC AS launcher
Two—triple Mk 32 AS torpedo tubes
Helicopter: One. No hangar

As with the closely similar, but later, *Belknaps* this is a nine-ship class. Again the reason was a Congressional stipulation for nuclear propulsion in one unit of the original plan and thus there is a close family likeness with the *Bainbridge* (CGN 25) with an armament strongly biased towards the missile. The primary recognition difference between the *Leahy* and *Belknap* classes is the additional twin Terrier launcher mounted aft in the former class, together with the associated pair of Mk 76 directors.

This 'double-ended' configuration gives the class

powerful AA capacity, ideal for a task force screen, but it is gained at the expense of surface armament. This is very weak, consisting of only four 3-inch guns, paired in open tubs at the after end of the superstructure.

The weakness in SSM's (Surface-to-Surface Missiles) has been a feature of US naval design which was heavily biased towards aircraft defence from one of its numerous carriers. As the handy-sized war-built carriers are being stricken, however, they are not being replaced and their diminishing numbers now render surface ships more vulnerable. (The Russians, by contrast, have never relied on seaborne air cover and have developed a useful range of SSM's which, while not perfect, pose a very real threat.)

To partly redress the imbalance, the Standard missile now entering service has been given an interim limited surface-to-surface capability. Being primarily an AA missile it has, however, aparabolic trajectory which makes it vulnerable to interception or jamming by ECM. The modern answer is the surface-skimming missile which is very hard to detect. The belated American weapon is the Harpoon which should begin to enter service in 1975. It should have a 35-mile range and be fired

No. CG16 *Leahy*

from an 8-tube 'pepperbox', slightly smaller than that of the ASROC.

The Terrier launchers on the *Leahy* class ships are of the Model 5 type which can fire Standard missiles. These are designed to replace the long line of Terriers; they are smaller, more robust and designed to seek their targets in spite of ECM. The Model 5 launcher does not fire the ASROC missile and a separate 'pepperbox' mounting is thus sited just forward of the bridge.

Owing to the different armament mix to the *Belknaps*, no space is available for a LAMPS helicopter. The after end of the superstructure is, therefore, lower in profile. A pad is provided on the quarterdeck but only minimal facilities and no hangar.

AS backup for the ASROC is the normal pair of triple Mk 32 torpedo tubes. These are sided on deck at the after end of the bridge structure and there is none fixed within the upperworks. They have the earlier SQS-23 sonar in the bow dome.

The quoted draught for the class is considerably less than that for the *Belknaps* which are of almost similar dimensions. It suggests a dome of greatly different configuration. The difficulties of leading anchors clear of this type of obstruction will probably lead to the more common adoption of the bottom-stowing variety which houses flush in a pocket on the underside of the ship.

All the class has undergone an AAW (Anti-Air Warfare) updating and their radar fit is now indistinguishable from that of the later *Belknaps*. The extra electronics required more space and the 'midships gap in the superstructure was plated-in giving a more 'built-up' appearance than that of their near sisters.

Belknap Guided Missile Frigate   United States

Units: No. CG 26 *Belknap*
No. CG 27 *Josephus Daniels*
No. CG 28 *Wainwright*
No. CG 29 *Jouett*
No. CG 30 *Horne*

No. CG 31 *Sterrett*
No. CG 32 *William H. Standly*
No. CG 33 *Fox*
No. CG 34 *Biddle*

	Belknap	Daniels	Wain-wright	Jouette	Horne	Sterrett	Standly	Fox	Biddle
Laid Down:	1962	1962	1962	1962	1962	1962	1963	1963	1963
Launched:	1963	1963	1964	1964	1964	1964	1964	1964	1965
Completed:	1964	1965	1966	1966	1967	1967	1966	1966	1967

Displacement: 6,600 standard
7,900 Deep Load
Length (o.a.): 547ft
Beam: 55ft
Draught: 29ft
Machinery: Geared steam turbines 2 shafts 85,000shp for 33 knots

Armament: One—twin Terrier SAM/ASROC launcher
One—5-inch DP gun
Two—3-inch AA guns (2 × 1)
Two—triple Mk 32 AS torpedo tubes
Helicopter: One

No. CG26 *Belknap*

The nine ships of this class are first cousins to the nuclear propelled *Truxtun* (CGN 35) but differ not only in their conventional machinery but also in the armament layout, the missile launcher being forward and the gun aft. They are excellent all-round ships but, as with all 'Western' ships, seem underarmed when compared with equivalent Russian designs, in this case with the smaller *Kresta II.* It is the price paid for higher standards of habitability.

The *Belknaps* are follow-ons to the *Leahys* with more emphasis placed on general-purpose capabilites. They resemble the earlier class quite closely although these can be identified by the second pair of Terrier directors and launcher mounted aft.

The after end of the *Belknaps* superstructure is much higher, housing as it does the LAMPS (Light Airborne Multi-Purpose System) helicopter which has replaced the second Terrier system. It seems strange that the *Belknap/Truxtun* group is the only one among US escorts with full facilities for a helicopter acting as a self-contained weapons system, the majority having only a pad and minimal facilities. LAMPS is built around the Kaman H-2 Seasprite helicopter, modified to the SH-2D configuration. It has manifold duties including extending the ship's early warning system, its AS sensors include dipping sonar, sonobuoys and magnetic anomaly detectors (MAD). It can carry a pair of AS torpedoes.

The site vacated by the earlier Terrier launcher aft has been taken by a 5-inch 54-calibre automatic DP gun whose director is sited atop the hangar. There are only two 3-inch guns to back it up, placed in single mountings in open tubs amidships.

The twin launcher forward in 'A' position is of the Model 7 variety loading either Terriers or ASROC missiles as programmed through the low, ramplike structure abaft it. When the Standard MR missile becomes more freely available, it will probably be modified to accept it. (See under *Leahy* class for more details.)

Closer range AS defence is covered by a triple bank of Mk 32 torpedo tubes on either side of the weather deck at the after end of the bridge structure. These replace a pair of fixed tubes formerly mounted in the superstructure below the helicopter pad and firing out over the beam. Attack data is augmented by the SQS-26 sonar housed in a prominent dome at the forefoot.

Radar antennae are supported on two large 'macks'. These are utilitarian rather than elegant, but provide solid structure for the sensitive electronics. Stack gases exit through ducts angled out near the tops of the towers. The arrangement is similar to that on gas-turbine propelled ships although these usually have structures of more generous proportions with more pronounced air-intakes.

All ships of the class feature an SPS-48 antenna on the foremast, supplying 3-dimensional data to the NTDS plot below. Above and abaft this antenna is the smaller SPS-10 search radar. A larger search array is mounted on the after 'mack', a large rectangular SPS-37 on CG 26-28 and a smaller curved SPS-40 on the remainder.

It will be noted that the low quarterdeck has been retained because the helicopter accommodation is in the superstructure rather than below decks.

Coontz Guided Missile Frigate

United States

Units: No. DDG 37 *Farragut*
No. DDG 38 *Luce* (ex-*Dewey*)
No. DDG 39 *Macdonough*
No. DDG 40 *Coontz*
No. DDG 41 *King*

No. DDG 42 *Mahan*
No. DDG 43 *Dahlgren*
No. DDG 44 *William V. Pratt*
No. DDG 45 *Dewey*
No. DDG 46 *Preble*

	Farragut	Luce	Mac-donough	Coontz	King	Mahan	Dahlgren	William V. Pratt	Dewey	Preble
Laid Down:	1957	1957	1958	1957	1957	1957	1958	1958	1957	1957
Launched:	1958	1958	1959	1958	1958	1959	1960	1960	1958	1959
Completed:	1960	1961	1961	1960	1960	1960	1961	1961	1959	1960

Displacement: 4,700 standard
5,800 Deep Load
Length (o.a.): 513ft
Beam: 53ft
Draught: 24ft
Machinery: Geared steam turbines 2 shafts 85,000shp for 33 knots
Armament: One—twin Terrier SAM launcher
One—5-inch DP gun
One—8-tube ASROC launcher
Two—triple Mk 32 AS torpedo tubes
Helicopter: Landing space for one. No hangar

Although formerly termed frigates, the *Coontz* class has the long sweeping sheerline, flush-decked hull and prominently capped funnels that betray a destroyer ancestry going back to the *Fletchers* of World War II. Stretched, missile-armed developments of the all-gun *Mitschers,* they were planned as an extended group of about 20 ships. During the construction period there were great improvements in design and the class was curtailed at 10, with the later units being re-vamped to become the completely separate *Leahy* class.

The *Coontz* class was the first group of American

No. DDG 37 *Farragut*

escorts designed from the outset as missile carriers and took the title 'frigate'. The numbering sequence commenced at DLG 6, as DLG 1-5 inclusive were allocated to the four large *Mitschers* and the lone *Norfolk*. All of these were due for missile conversions but only two were finally fitted with Tartar and these were redesignated DDG. From July 1975, DLG 6-15 were reclassified DDG 37-46, i.e. Destroyers, guided missile.

In contrast to the 'macks' of later classes, the *Coontz*'s retain separate funnels and masts although the size and burdens borne by the latter show why the 'mack' made sense.

Armament layout is that now most favoured for a 'single ender', i.e. launcher aft. The first five carried the RIM-2D beam-riding version of the Terrier and the last five the RIM-2F semi-active homing version, suggesting that the long range 'kill' was then considered more important than at present, when the single, low-flying target is the major threat.

A single 5-inch, 54-calibre DP gun is shipped in 'A' position inferior to an 8-tube ASROC launcher in 'B'. *Farragut* alone has a sloping extension to the bridge front, containing a modified ASROC reloading system.

Originally, four 3-inch 50's were paired in tubs abaft the after funnel but these were landed in the course of an anti-air warfare (AAW) conversion. This refit improved fire-control arrangements and reduced reaction time, making it possible for the Standard MR missile to be eventually deployed. NTDS's (Naval Tactical Data Systems) which were first evaluated in two of the class, were fitted to all. Improvements in the electronic fit have necessitated increasing the size of the superstructure, particularly aft. Aluminium has been used to compensate.

On updating, an SPS-48 antenna is fitted on the foremast and an SPS-37 on the tower-like mainmast together with a TACAN pod. All have the SQS-23 sonar although, judging by the conventionally sited anchors, this is probably mounted in a keel dome rather than at the forefoot.

The quarterdeck is marked out with a helicopter pad, but no hangar is provided and facilities are minimal.

King was fitted with a Vulcan-Phalanx Close-in Weapons System (CIWS) for an evaluation period. This system (also developed by the Russians around their 37mm gun) is designed as a 'last-ditch' defence against incoming missiles that have not been successfully intercepted or jammed. It works on the Gatling principle of multiple 20mm barrels rotating with a common feed system, giving an extremely high rate of fire which is supposed to saturate with fragments the air space through which the missile has to pass, upsetting the guidance system or detonating it.

A new, light-weight 8-inch gun is under development, which could give the smaller ship greater conventional firepower, but it is difficult to see its role vis-a-vis the Harpoon SSM which will probably be fired from the ASROC launcher when it enters service.

Spruance Guided Missile Destroyer   United States

Units: No. DD 963 *Spruance*
No. DD 964 *Paul F. Foster*
No. DD 965 *Kincaid*
No. DD 966 *Hewitt*
No. DD 967 *Elliott*
No. DD 968 *Arthur W. Radford*
No. DD 969 *Peterson*

No. DD 970 *Caron*
No. DD 971 *David R. Ray*
No. DD 972 *Oldendorf*
No. DD 973 *John Young*
No. DD 974 *Comte de Grasse*
No. DD 975-85
No. DD 986-92 proposed

	Spruance	Paul F. Foster	Kincaid	Hewitt	Elliott	Arthur W. Radford	Peterson	Caron	David R. Ray	Oldendorf	John Young	Comte de Grasse	975-8	979-85	986-92 Proposed
Laid Down:	1972	1973	1973	1973	1973	1974	1974	1974	1974	1974	1975	1975	1975	—	—
Launched:	1973	1974	1974	1974	1974	1974	1975	1975	1975	1975	1975	1975	1975	—	—
Completed:	1975	1975	1975	1975	1975	1976	1975	1976	1976	1976	1976	1976	1976	by 1978	

Displacement: 8,000 Deep Load
Length (o.a.): 563ft
Beam: 55ft
Draught: 29ft
Machinery: Four gas turbines on 2 shafts 8,000shp for 31 knots

Armament: Two—5-inch (Mk 45) DP (2 × 1)
One—BPDMS Sea Sparrow launcher
One—ASROC AS launcher
Two—triple Mk 32 AS torpedo tubes
Helicopter: One LAMPS

No. DD963 *Spruance*

The US Navy, expanded rapidly during the years of war, found itself in 1945 with a large number of modern destroyers. With this armada available, only limited new construction was undertaken during the following years and the problem of eventual block obsolescence was recognised. This was delayed in the 'sixties by an extended programme of modifications (FRAM I and II) designed to extend their useful lives. On the approach of the end of this extension a new 'DX' project was initiated to produce a general purpose design to replace the versatile destroyer.

Thus emerged the controversial DD 963 or *Spruance* class, which is also the first American essay into gas turbine propulsion for major warships.

The controversy is centred around the apparent lack of punch in a ship that approaches 8,000 tons. In size, the *Spruances* are equivalent to the Russian *Kresta II*'s which mount an SSM and two SAM Systems designed to engage both high and low altitude targets. The *Spruance* has only the BPDMS Sea Sparrow with a range of less than 10 miles. Any aerial target penetrating this line of defence has to be countered by a pair of CIWS Vulcan/Phalanx guns.

In fairness to the design it is meant to have an AS bias and this is dependent upon the ASROC launcher forward of the bridge, two triple Mk 32 torpedo tube banks and a LAMPS helicopter system—but all this was also incorporated in the similarly-sized *Belknap* class (q.v.) which managed a long range SAM system in addition. A slight edge is given to the newer design in that the SH-2 Seasprite helicopter could be replaced by the

larger, and more effective SH-3 Sea King; there i also provision aft for an SQS-VDS, but there i doubt if this will be fitted as the ships also have th highly effective SQS-53 in a bulb forward.

Two 5-inch guns of the new lightweight Mk 4 design are fitted. The saving in weight an manpower of these automatic DP weapons i rather offset by a lower rate of fire and lowe elevation than earlier models.

This limited surface-to-surface capability coul well be supplemented by the eventual launching o the Harpoon missile from the ASROC 'pepperbox'

The hull is long forecastle deck form with a sho quarterdeck; a long graceful sheerline terminates i an aggressively raked bow.

The large-section funnels demanded by ga turbines have rendered the usual 'macks' impractic able and two lattice masts of distinctly unlovel aspect alternate with the funnels in an arrangemen reminiscent of the British County class. The stack are, however, rectangular in section and staggere in a layout which probably conforms to that of th machinery spaces. The superstructure is high, box and rather featureless, terminating at the after en with a sudden drop at the helicopter hangar. Th pad for the helicopter is one level higher than migh be expected, possibly to counteract the blast effec from the Sea Sparrow launcher close abaft it.

'Up top' the electronic fit lacks the familia rectangular SPS-48 antenna which normally woul give 3-D information for a longer ranged SAM system. Production of the class is in a 'ship facility with much usebeing made of pre-fabricatio techniques.

Tarawa Amphibious Assault Ship

United State

Units: No. LHA 1 *Tarawa*
No. LHA 2 *Saipan*
No. LHA 3 *Da Nang*
No. LHA 4 *Belleau Wood*
No. LHA 5 *Nassau*

	Tarawa	Saipan	Da Nang	Belleau Wood	Nassau
Laid Down:	1971	1972	1973	1973	1974
Launched:	1973	1974	1974	1975	1975
Completed:	1975	1975	1976	1976	1976

Displacement: 40,000 Deep Load
Length (o.a.): 820ft
Beam: 106ft
Draught: 28ft
Machinery: Geared steam turbines 2 shafts 70,000shp for c. 23 knots
Armament: Two—BPDMS Sea Sparrow SAM launchers
Three—5-inch DP guns (3 × 1)
Aircraft: 28-32 helicopters dependent upon mix of transport, support and observation types. Mainly UH-46 Sea Knight and CH-53 Sea Stallion.
Possibly some AV-8A *Harrier* type V/STOL in lieu of partial helicopter capacity
Cancelled: LHA 6-9 (1971)

The chunky profile of this design belies its size looking at first sight like an escort carrier, it is i fact, well over 800 feet in length. An exceedingl ambitious concept it seeks to combine th functions of the Amphibious Assault Ships of th *Iwo Jima* class (LPH) and the Amphibiou Transport Docks of the *Austin* and *Raleigh* classe (LPD) and offering in addition a large carg capacity.

By accepting the risks of an 'all eggs in on basket' approach, certain advantages are to b gained. Within one hull there are nearly 2,000 fully equipped troops with their transport, armour an heavy weapons, together with the means of gettin them ashore and keeping them supported for considerable length of time.

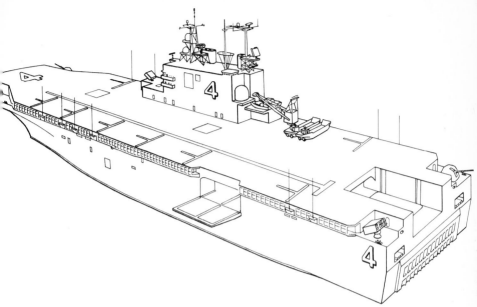

No. LHA 1 *Tarawa*

The hull is very carrier-like in profile, with a high freeboard and a prominent knuckle forward. It is virtually parallel-bodied from the after end of the forward entry to the transom, which is squared-off and incorporates a half-height docking gate.

A large, box-like island with two squat funnels is set on the starboard side of the full-sized flight deck, which is geared for helicopter operation and without catapults or arrestor grear. Below either side of the flight deck edge is a prominent walkway which enables troops to reach their helicopters rapidly without having to cross the flight deck.

Below the after half of the flight deck is the helicopter hangar with interconnection by two elevators, one on the centre line above the docking gate and one on the port deck edge about 200 feet further forward.

Below the forward part of the flight deck are stores areas, with small elevators permitting their rapid transfer up to the waiting helicopters.

Below this stores area is the garage space for armour, large weaponry and transport with access leading aft into the docking area below the hangar where they can be loaded into the embarked LCU's (Landing Craft, Utility). Four of the 1610 Type can be embarked in this dock, which occupies one-third of the ship's length. They are 135 feet in length and are capable of putting ashore three medium tanks or about 170 tons of cargo.

The comparatively deep draught of the mother ship means that little trimming will be necessary for docking operations although the low headroom of the sterngate could cause a little trouble in a heavy swell. To assist in keeping the ship aligned to weather during this operation, a powerful side thruster is fitted forward in a transverse tunnel.

No smaller LCVP's are at present carried in davits, but a heavy crane is sited abaft the superstructure with duties that include the placing overside of small assault craft carried on the flight deck.

A pocket for defensive armament is recessed into each corner of the flight deck. Three of these will house single 5-inch 54 DP guns and the port quarter position will have a BPDMS Sea Sparrow launcher. A second of these 'pepperboxes' will be sited on a forward extension of the island.

The ten-ship series (four have since been cancelled) made it worthwhile for the builders to construct a special 'ship facility' where production-line methods could be used to pre-fabricate the modules from which the ships will be built.

Iwo Jima Amphibious Assault Ship   United States

Units: No. LPH 2 *Iwo Jima*
No. LPH 3 *Okinawa*
No. LPH 7 *Guadalcanal*
No. LPH 10 *Tripoli*
No. LPH 11 *New Orleans*
No. LPH 12 *Inchon*

	Iwo Jima	*Okinawa*	*Guadalcanal*	*Tripoli*	*New Orleans*	*Inchon*
Laid Down:	1959	1960	1961	1964	1966	1968
Launched:	1960	1961	1963	1965	1968	1969
Completed:	1961	1962	1963	1966	1968	1970

Displacement: 17,000 standard
18,300 Deep Load
Length (o.a.): 602ft
Beam: 84ft
Draught: 27ft
Machinery: Geared steam turbine 1 shaft
23,000shp for 20 knots
Armament: Two — BPDMS Sea Sparrow launchers
Four — 3-inch 50-calibre AA guns (2 × 2)
Aircraft: About 30 helicopters dependent upon mix

For other of same class, see:
Guam

This group of seven (including *Guam*, LPH 9 (q.v.)) was the first purpose-built class of amphibious assault ship. With over 2,000 marines embarked they correspond closely in function to the British *Hermes* (q.v.) but differ in relying entirely upon helicopters to put the force ashore and support it. This, however, is by policy rather than by limitations in the design, as shown by *Inchon* which has been fitted with sponsons on either side aft, each bearing an LCVP which is housed under a heavy gantry-type davit.

As the principles of operation of the SCS are at present being developed by the *Guam*, so were those of the LPH proved by interim modifications. These were of *Essex* and *Commencement Bay* class carriers and which, now discarded, account for the non-consecutive pennant numbers of the *Iwo Jimas*.

Although the overall appearance is that of an aircraft carrier, the class has no designed capability in this direction, being fitted with neither catapults nor arrestor gear.

The *Guam* exercise has demonstrated that they can switch roles without great trouble and, if the SCS project is finally axed, the whole class could be similarly converted.

The lack of catapults forward has resulted in a characteristic round forward end to the flight deck, which is marked for helicopter operations only. As these are essentially vertical in nature, there is no flight path, the deck being laid out with seven pads to port and parking and loading space to starboard. Angling of the flight deck was not necessary.

Helicopter access from hangar to flight deck is through two deck-edge elevators. That on the port side is opposite the forward end of the island and that to starboard abaft the island. Both elevators are capable of hingeing up from the 'down' position, resting against the ship's side and obviating the need for hull doors. Helicopter stores are brought topside by two smaller elevators, set inboard.

The bridge structure is very angular in profile, with a small, square funnel set well back. Atop the island is a tapered pole mast with a TACAN pod at the truck and an SPS-10 antenna below. The larger aerial of the SPS-40 search radar is mounted on a short lattice tower above the bridge, and several have a prominent dome at the after end of the island which houses a Carrier Control Approach (CCA) antenna. As their operation involves spending a considerable time within helicopter range of an enemy, the LPH's could well be prime targets for shore-based missiles and are equipped with extensive ECM gear for protection.

The original armament was eight 3-inch 50's, paired in twos on either quarter and in superfiring positions forward of the island. The latter mounts were enclosed on *New Orleans* and *Inchon* only. To give better close-in protection, two BPDMS Sea Sparrow launchers have since been fitted, one in place of the portquarter 3-inch mounting and the other in place of the lower 3-inch position forward of the superstructure.

Helicopter mix depends largely upon the mission of the individual ship. Typically, it would include a flight of CH-46 Sea Knights. Versatile, double-rotor units, they are capable not only of transport and AS work but also of towing mine-sweeping gear; successfully demonstrated at Haiphong and Suez. CH 53 Sea Stallions are used for heavy cargo or troop movements and UH-1 Bell Hueys for support. There will be no more of this type of ship as its functions are now being included in those of the *Tarawa* class LHA's.

No. LPH 2 *Iwo Jima*

Proposed Sea Control Ship

United States

No	Commission
A	1978
B, C and D	1979
E and F	1980
G and H	1981

Displacement: 15,000 Deep Load
Length (o.a.): 650ft
Beam: 80ft
Draught: 22ft
Width: 105ft (over flight deck)
Machinery: Two gas turbines 1 shaft
40,000shp for c. 26 knots
Armament: Two—CIWS Vulcan/Phalanx 20mm
guns or
Two—BPDMS Sea Sparrow missile systems
Aircraft: Three—AV-8 V/STOL equivalents
Fourteen—SH-3 Sea King helicopter equivalents

Note: *Final classification may be CH (Helicopter Cruiser)*

One of the most successful ship designs of World War II was the Escort Carrier. Simple and inexpensive, she possessed virtually no offensive power but her aircraft. Properly escorted, however, she could establish a local air superiority to provide an umbrella for groups of ships otherwise exposed to attack. Since the war, most ship designs have become complex and expensive due, in great measure, to a multi-function approach and a strong argument can be made for return to 'pure' designs, with an acceptance of their limitations in view of their cheapness and smaller complements.

It is claimed that the SCS, or Sea Control Ship, is an entirely new type of vessel and definitely not a carrier, but her functions really parallel those of the old escort carrier quite closely. With minimal on-board means of self-protection, her aircraft would operate in AS, or AA or airborne early warning (AEW)/defence co-ordination modes.

The design, like that of the British *Invincible*, was triggered by the development of a successful V/STOL aircraft.

Both ships are about 650 feet in length and make an interesting comparison. *Invincible* is armed offensively and is designed to operate as such as part of a group; her aircraft mix would probably be of the order of nine Sea King type helicopters and six V/STOL strike aircraft such as the Harrier. The SCS on the other hand, has a more specialised role to play which is primarily defensive and this is reflected by her expected mix of sixteen helicopters and only three AV-8 Harrier equivalents.

Her value to a group that she accompanies would be greatly enhanced by her ability to operate, service and, if necessary, replace LAMPS helicopters. This is a vital requirement for those escorts whose AS capabilities are geared to the helicopter but whose maintenance facilities are limited.

Although the design is far from finalised, official models show the SCS as being an orthodox small carrier in profile except that the flight deck terminates some 70 feet from the stern, giving a low quarterdeck. From this level there is access to the after end of the hangar through a large door and there is a large deckedge elevator at this break. A second elevator is to starboard of the centreline forward of the island. The flight deck is moderately angled, but in the opposite sense to normal practice, i.e. the aircraft approach is to the port side

of the after elevator and angles over to starboard. This is possible because neither arrestor wires nor catapults are fitted. By this means, most of the limited flightpath of an STOL aircraft is within the envelope of the ship and sponsoning is minimal.

The island is boxy and has a basic range of radars including search and approach control sets. The large funnel and prominent air intakes betray her gas turbine propulsion. It is planned to have two low-powered versions of this compact prime-mover driving on to a single shaft with a controllable pitch propeller to obviate need of reversal. For cruising, only one gas turbine would be used, running at rated output; this is more efficient than having two

running at lower speeds. The second unit can be rapidly clutched-in when necessary. This will boost rapidly to the comparitively modest top speed of 26 knots.

Defensive armament has not been fixed but would probably include both BPDMS Sea Sparrows and the CIWS Phalanx. No sonar is fitted as the helicopter complement can perform its own detection duties.

By keeping to an uncomplicated specification, the US Navy hopes to have eight SCS's in operation by 1981 at a total cost less than that of the new CVN 70 alone.

Guam Interim Sea Control Ship

United States

Units: No. LPH 9 *Guam*
Laid Down: 1962
Launched: 1964
Completed: 1965
Displacement: 18,300 Deep Load
Length (o.a.): 602ft
Beam: 84ft
Draught: 104ft
Machinery: One geared steam turbine 1 shaft 23,000shp for 21 knots
Armament: Two—BPDMS Sea Sparrow Missile systems
Four—3-inch AA guns (2 × 2)
Aircraft: Six—AV-8 Harrier V/STOL equivalents
SH-2F Kaman Seasprite AS helicopter Total about
SH-3H Sikorsky Sea King AS helicopter eight

See also
Iwo Jima class

Originally a unit of the *Iwo Jima* class (q.v.) of Amphibious Assault Ship, *Guam* was modified in 1971-2 to evaluate the concept of the Sea Control Ship. She is now officially rated as Interim SCS although modifications were not sufficient to warrant a change in her LPH designation. The primary change was in the aircraft mix, where she landed the 30-odd mixed helicopter force and embarked a section of about six AV-8 Harrier V/STOL aircraft and about eight helicopters. The latter are SH-3H Sea Kings and SH-2F Sea Sprites, the type used on LAMPS escorts. This force is far better geared to air superiority and AS work than the earlier mix of heavy assault, transport and observation units.

These helicopters would be expected to provide a protective aerial umbrella over a group of ships such as a convoy, replenishment group or small assault force operating in a 'low-threat' combat

area. She is not expected to defend herself or her group against say, a carrier strike. The versatile helicopter is used, however, not just in an AS mode but can deploy air-to-air and air-to-surface missiles if required and give long range early warning.

The interesting part will be the use of the Harriers. Although subsonic, they have a fast reaction time from their carrier which does not need to work up speed or steam head-to-wind. They would be a potent answer to an aircraft performing a mid-course correction on a missile fired from a ship below the horizon and have the capability of going on to strike the ship herself. They have proved very useful in laying sonobuoys, being at the scene far quicker than the helicopters, which can follow in for an attack on the submerged target.

Harriers are VTOL capable but have a far greater range and/or payload if given STOL facilities. LPH's resemble small aircraft carriers but are geared to helicopters, i.e. vertical aircraft operation rather than horizontal. Guam's conversion, therefore, was concerned in giving her some of the features of an aircraft carrier, with a modified flight deck layout and lighting, and the installation of

Carrier-Control Approach (CCA) radar, housed in the dome at the after end of the superstructure. The new flight-path layout was facilitated by the situation of both elevators at the deckedge. Different maintenance facilities were built-in together with a new tactical command centre, geared to operations not previously the preserve of an LPH.

Although the deck required little reinforcement, with the take-off weight of an AV-8A some eleven tons compared with the nineteen tons of the Sikorsky CH-53 Sea Stallions previously embarked, the jet efflux of the former when used in the VTOL mode can produce severe local heating problems, necessitating special take-off pads.

During the conversion, four of the original eight 3-inch guns were landed in favour of two BPDMS Sea Sparrow launchers.

Should the planned SCS class become a reality, Guam will probably revert to an orthodox LPH, but if the project were to be axed, then the whole Iwo Jima class could be converted to an SCS role, as their original functions will be largely usurped by the new Tarawa-class LHA's (q.v.).

Austin Amphibious Transport Dock   United States

Units: No. LPD 4 *Austin*
No. LPD 5 *Ogden*
No. LPD 6 *Duluth*
No. LPD 7 *Cleveland*
No. LPD 8 *Dubuque*
No. LPD 9 *Denver*

No. LPD 10 *Juneau*
No. LPD 11 *Coronado*
No. LPD 12 *Shreveport*
No. LPD 13 *Nashville*
No. LPD 14 *Trenton*
No. LPD 15 *Ponce*

	Austin	*Ogden*	*Duluth*	*Cleveland*	*Dubuque*	*Denver*	*Juneau*	*Coronado*	*Shreveport*	*Nashville*	*Trenton*	*Ponce*
Laid Down:	1963	1963	1963	1964	1965	1964	1965	1965	1965	1966	1966	1966
Launched:	1964	1964	1965	1966	1966	1965	1966	1966	1966	1967	1968	1970
Completed:	1965	1965	1966	1967	1967	1968	1969	1970	1970	1970	1971	1971

Displacement: 10,000 standard
16,900 Deep Load
Length (o.a.): 569ft
Beam: 84ft
Draught: 22ft
Machinery: Geared steam turbines 2 shafts
24,000shp for 21 knots
Armament: Eight—3-inch AA (4 × 2)
Helicopters: Six heavy (UH-34 Sikorsky Seabat/ Seashore or later CH-46 Boeing-Vetol Sea Knight)
Cancelled: LPD 16 (1969)
See also *Raleigh* class

The twelve *Austins* are virtually identical in appearance with the pair of *Raleighs* (q.v.) of a slightly earlier deate. They are, however, longer with a 50-foot section added forward of the docking area, devoted to extra stowage space for vehicles and stores.

Identification between the two classes is not

easy, the only sure way being through the hull number. Should this not be visible, the funnel positions also differ slightly although as these are sided and staggered, with the starboard the more forward, it is not obvious from some angles, particularly as a prominent crane post is sited directly abaft the starboard funnel. There are twin 3-inch gun tubs sited abaft the bridge in both classes; the *Raleighs* have the starboard funnel forward and the *Austins* have it abaft its adjacent 3-inch mount. Thus in a beam profile of the *Austins*, the funnels are closer together.

The most immediate impression is that of high freeboard, particularly in relation to the long bridge structure which appears low, although rising three further decks above the forecastle and flight deck, which are at the same level. The combination of freeboard and flare has resulted in a long curving knuckle forward which pleasantly offsets the otherwise featureless hull.

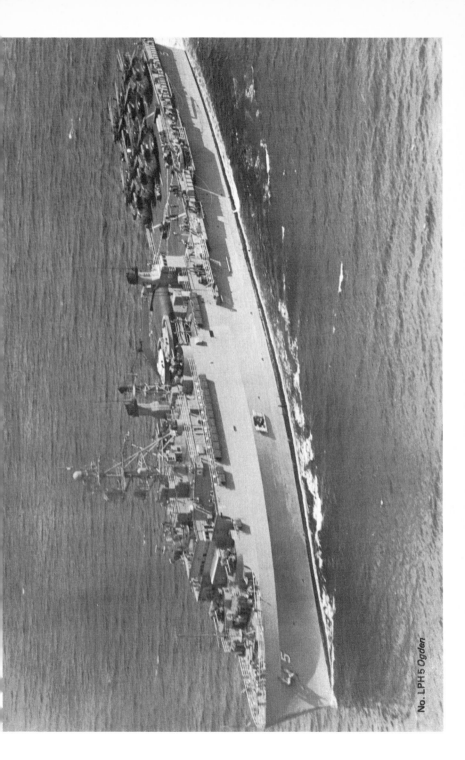

No. LPH 5 *Ogden*

A large lattice mast tops the bridge house, bearing an SPS-40 search and other navigation antennae, together with pods for TACAN and ECM equipment.

The long, featureless flight deck runs right to the square transom and permanently bridges in the docking area. This space is much smaller than in equivalently-sized LSD's, giving more space forward. This is devoted largely to accommodation for some 900 troops (some 100 less than in the *Raleighs*) together with their stores and transport. LPD7-13 inclusive carry less troops but offer accommodation for a flag officer and staff, which gives them the ability to act as command ships in a limited situation.

Careful thought has been given to 'cargo flow' and the inclusion of mercantile-style side ports in the hull permits wheeled traffic to 'roll-on' and reduces parking problems once aboard. Ramps interconnect the stores area with both flight deck and dock.

An LCU (Landing Craft, Utility) can be stowed on one side of the dock, leaving room for three LCM 6 craft in a nose-to-tail line, on the other side. Stores other than wheeled traffic can be 'spotted' into any of the craft by means of overhead gantry cranes.

The LCM's can alternatively ferry about 80 equipped men if necessary, although this task is normally the province of the LCPL's which are nested on the upper deck between the funnels and handled by the prominent crane, which normally stows athwartships.

Movement ashore by water is, however, only supplementary to the rapid discharge by helicopter from the large flight deck. Helicopters are normally those belonging to other ships in company but several of the class are now fitted with a telescopic hangar which opens out along tracks and is large enough to provide temporary housing for a heavy helicopter.

These flexible ships have also proved very useful in the helicopter-minesweeping role. No more are planned as the majority of their functions can be performed by the new *Tarawa* class LHA's (q.v.).

Raleigh Amphibious Transport Dock

United States

Units: No. LPD 1 *Raleigh*
No. LPD 2 *Vancouver*
No. AGF 3 *La Salle* (ex-LPD 3)

	Raleigh	Vancouver	La Salle
Laid Down:	1960	1960	1962
Launched:	1962	1962	1963
Completed:	1962	1963	1964

Displacement: 8,100 standard
14,600 Deep Load
Length (o.a.): 522ft
Beam: 84ft
Draught: 22ft
Machinery: Steam turbines 2 shafts 24,000shp for 20 knots
Armament: Eight—3-inch AA (4 × 2)
Helicopters: Six heavy (UH-34 Sikorsky Seabat/ Seahorse or the later CH-46 Boeing-Vertol Sea Knight)
No hangar

See also *Austin* class

The small number of units in this class probably resulted from the realisation that the design could easily be 'stretched' to give greater capacity. They were, therefore, limited to only three and the series continued as the very similar *Austin* class.

The *Raleighs* were, nevertheless, the first attempt at an Amphibious Transport Dock, or LPD and, like other designs in this area, are an amalgam of earlier types, each of which had limitations in certain directions.

First, there was the Dock Landing Ship, or LSD (e.g. *Anchorage* class). This type has the ability to operate a wide range of small landing craft but lacks the accommodation necessary for the considerable force of troops which should be carried if she is to realise her full potential when working alone.

Secondly, there were the closely related classes of Amphibious Transport (LPA) and Amphibious Cargo Ships (LKA), neither of which are within the scope of this book.

The LPA's are based on the well-proven standard C-2 merchant hulls (*Haskell* class, seven extant, all in reserve) and the later and much more advanced C4-Mariner hulls (*Paul Revere* class, two extant, both active). The latter type are 22-knot ships and a very successful design. The LPA's embody a good troop-carrying capacity, with the C4's accommodating over 1,600. Limitations exist inevitably on the means of putting them ashore. The size of the landing craft is governed by what can be slung under davits or put over the side by the ship's heavy cargo-handling gear. The craft are stowed athwartships across the reinforced hatch covers and off-loading them in any sea is a difficult task.

The LKA's operate similarly but are involved primarily in the carriage of stores, although limited troop capacity is provided. The fine new ships of the *Charleston* class can handle a large helicopter and 18 LCM's are carried topsides.

The *Raleigh* class seeks to combine the functions of all three types in one hull although the 14,000 tons limit obviously means that it cannot have the capacities of any of the individual specialist ships.

Although very similar to the LSD in profile, the extra accommodation of the LPD gives her a rather more 'built-up' appearance forward. The flight deck runs the full length of the docking area below and terminates at the sterngate, thus leaving no characteristic step in the profile as on the LSD. This extra deck area has permitted the marking of two helicopter pads.

A telescopic hangar has been fitted to LPD 1 and 2, similar to that on the *Austins*. As the class would normally work as part of a balanced force, probably including an Amphibious Assault Ship, helicopters

No. LPD 1 *Raleigh*

would be available, so none is usually supplied as part of the ship's establishment.

La Salle has been re-classified a Miscellaneous Command Ship (AGF), and has been modified to serve as a flagship to US naval forces in the Indian Ocean and the Gulf.

An extra accommodation deck was built topsides with a small communications mast on the port side. A large temporary deckhouse occupies much of the forward flight deck area and the ship has been painted white to reduce heat effects. See also *Austin* class notes.

Anchorage Landing Ship Dock

United States

Units: No. LSD 36 *Anchorage*
No. LSD 37 *Portland*
No. LSD 38 *Pensacola*
No. LSD 39 *Mount Vernon*
No. LSD 40 *Fort Fisher*

	Anchorage	Portland	Pensacola	Mount Vernon	Fort Fisher
Laid Down.	1967	1967	1969	1970	1970
Launched:	1968	1969	1970	1971	1972
Completed:	1969	1970	1971	1972	1972

Displacement: 8,600 standard
13,700 Deep Load
Length (o.a.): 555ft
Beam: 84ft
Draught: 18ft
Machinery: Geared steam turbines 2 shafts
24,000shp for 20 knots
Armament: Eight—3-inch AA (4 × 2)
Helicopters: Double pad. No hangar

The Landing Ship, Dock (LSD) is the immediate ancestor of the LPD and, as their functions overlap to a certain extent, their appearance is quite similar. The immediate impression is that of a lower ship with a larger gap between the sided funnels; the flight deck does not cover the complete length of the docking area and ends short of the sterngate, giving a very characteristic step in the upper line of the profile.

No. LSD 36 *Anchorage*

Where the later LPD has also to act as a fairly comprehensive transport, the LSD's main task is to carry minor landing craft, docking and servicing them as necessary. The docking area is thus on a much more generous scale with a similar-sized hull, the well is about 430 feet in length, about 2½ times as large. This enables three of the larger 135-foot LCU's (1610 series) to be docked simultaneously. With a width of 50 feet, the dock could theoretically handle a line of LCM 6's as well, although these are not normally carried.

There is accommodation for about 400 troops but there are not the large transport parks and interconnecting deck ramps of the LPD, so there is greater emphasis on loading 'over the top'. There are, thus, two 50-ton capacity cranes sided amidships; they have jibs of open construction (one box-sectioned crane on LPD's) and the after (starboard) unit is capable of plumbing a large part of the dock area.

Because of this requirement the flight deck is not permanent, being little more than an elevated platform which acts as a movable bridge between the sides of the hull. It provides no cover or anything more than minimum facilities, but is large enough to operate a heavy helicopter such as a Sea Knight. This light deck is continued as far forward

as the after funnel and provides useful parking and handling space. Forward of this, as far as the bridge, the dock is open to the sky, being spanned by no more than a removable fore-and-aft brow. Either crane can operate through this aperture to work landing craft below.

Small landing craft are also carried topside; what is stowed varies from ship to ship and depends upon her mission but, typically, there is an LCM 6 which is lowered by crane and a large LCP and an LCVP in davits. These can, obviously, be supplemented if necessary.

Armament is on a light defensive scale, being only eight 3-inch 50's which are twinned at each corner of the bridge structure. The mountings forward are enclosed, unlike those on earlier classes and have rather restricted arcs, there being a communications mast on the forecastle. There are no missiles.

The *Anchorages* were designed to the recent requirement of a 20-knot minimum speed and replaced the elderly *Casa Grande* class (q.v.) and such of the earlier *Ashlands* as remained. Considering that they date some 15 years after the immediately preceding class of *Thomastons*, the design has remained remarkably unchanged. Radar fits are on the same scale as the *Raleighs*.

Thomaston Landing Ship Dock

United States

Units: No. LSD 28 *Thomaston*
No. LSD 29 *Plymouth Rock*
No. LSD 30 *Fort Snelling*
No. LSD 31 *Point Defiance*

No. LSD 32 *Spiegel Grove*
No. LSD 33 *Alamo*
No. LSD 34 *Hermitage*
No. LSD 35 *Monticello*

	Thomaston	*Plymouth Rock*	*Fort Snelling*	*Point Defiance*	*Spiegel Grove*	*Alamo*	*Hermitage*	*Monticello*
Laid Down:	1952	1953	1953	1953	1954	1954	1955	1955
Launched:	1954	1954	1954	1954	1955	1956	1956	1956
Completed:	1954	1955	1955	1955	1956	1956	1956	1957

Displacement: 6,900 standard
11,500 Deep Load
Length (o.a.): 510ft
Beam: 84ft
Draught: 20ft
Machinery: Steam turbines 2 shafts
24,000shp for 22 knots
Armament: Twelve—3-inch AA (6 × 2)
Helicopter: Single pad. No hangar

This group of eight represents a mid-point in the smooth evolution of the LSD from the war-built *Casa Grandes* to the latest class of *Anchorages*. From the point of view of recognition, they have their pair of heavy cranes sided almost opposite each other, as in the earlier classes but the funnels sided and staggered as in the later. The funnels themselves have had prominent black-painted extensions added to avoid down-draught problems,

and their positions indicate that the machinery spaces are not only split but also echeloned, giving a better chance of engine power remaining after severe action damage. The class retains the simple pole mast of the earlier designs, bearing a modest and rather dated radar fit. Being one deck lower than the *Anchorages* the hull has the prominent forward knuckle running aft from forecastle deck level; they are smaller ships, some 40 feet shorter, lower and not as weatherly.

The design dates from the early 'fifties, when it was customary to mount rather more guns than at present. Originally, the class had no less than sixteen 3-inch 50's and a few Oerlikons. The heavier guns were twinned and mounted in open tubs, two forward of the bridge structure, two each side (abaft the bridge)—some units have these on different levels, dependent upon the length of the deck above—and one on either dock wall aft. These

No. LSD 28 *Thomaston*

after mountings have since been removed together with the 20mm weapons. The gun directors are mounted on low bases on the bridge, fore and aft of the mast, on the centreline.

Amphibious craft as large as an LCM 6 are not normally carried topside although there are heavy gantry davits adjacent to the cranes, which handle double-tiered LCVP's.

The docking well, at over 400 feet, occupies about the same proportion of length as in the later class and is just long enough to accept three of the 1610 class LCU's (although the smaller 120-foot LCU 1466 type would be less of a tight fit). Alternatively, a small armada of eighteen LCM6's can be accommodated which can be increased to 21 in an emergency. These craft are pre-loaded as there is no internal ramp and storage space system on the scale of later designs. An intermediate, or mezzanine, deck can be fitted (after the fashion of modern car ferries which carry vehicles of low

height) and various small craft can be stowed here in addition, being probably handled by crane as it is unlikely that the ship could flood-down far enough to float them in.

To give greater flexibility to the cranes, the helicopter deck spanning the dock area is again removable. When in position, it ends well short of the sterngate to allow stowage of small craft with a large airdraught and extends forward into a parking/handling area and leaving an aperture abaft the bridge to allow the cranes to plumb the dock below.

Twin steam turbines of the same power as the larger and later class give the class a two-knot advantage. They have a slightly smaller troop capacity.

All eight were constructed in the same yard to gain the advantages of series production.

Casa Grande Landing Ship Dock

United States

Units: No. LSD 13 *Casa Grande*
No. LSD 14 *Rushmore*
No. LSD 15 *Shadwell*
No. LSD 16 *Cabildo*
No. LSD 17 *Catamount*
No. LSD 18 *Colonial*

No. LSD 19 *Comstock*
No. LSD 20 *Donner*
No. LSD 22 *Fort Marion*
No. LSD 26 *Tortuga*
No. LSD 27 *Whetstone*

No. LSD 13 *Casa Grande*

	Casa Grande	Rushmore	Shadwell	Cabildo	Catamount	Colonial	Comstock	Donner	Fort Marion	Tortuga	Whetstone
Laid Down:	1943	1943	1943	1943	1943	1943	1944	1944	1944	1944	1944
Launched:	1944	1944	1944	1944	1945	1945	1945	1945	1945	1945	1945
Completed:	1944	1944	1944	1945	1945	1945	1945	1945	1946	1945	1946

Displacement: 4,800 standard
9,400 Deep Load
Length (o.a.): 458ft
Beam: 76ft
Draught: 18ft
Machinery: Steam turbines 2 shafts
7,000shp for 16 knots
(LSD 22 only 9,000shp for 17 knots)
Armament: Four—40mm (LSD 22) (2 × 2)
Eight—40mm (LSD 13, 14 and 15) (2 × 4)
Twelve—40mm (2 × 4) + (2 × 2) in remainder
Disposals: LSD 9-12) inclusive to RN on completion
LSD 17 *Catamount* reported transferred to Israel 1976, new name and number unknown
LSD 21 ex-*Fort Mandan* now Greek *Nafkratoussa*
LSD 22 *Fort Marion* transferred to Taiwan 1975, new name and number unknown
LSD 23 *Fort Snelling* } cancelled 1945
LSD 24 *Point Defiance* }
LSD 25 ex-*San Marcos* now Spanish *Galicia*

Once the importance of amphibious capability had been grasped early in World War II there was an urgent need to produce the specialised ships required. The shortest route was by conversion of such ships as cross-channel ferries or good quality cargo liners.

Putting a fully-equipped combat unit onto a beach far removed from conventional ports required fast ships with (i) adequate troop accommodation, (ii) storage space for equipment, including transport and (iii) the small craft to ferry it ashore.

Conversion of standard tonnage realised, (i) easily, (ii) little stowage problem but difficulties in putting it ashore and (iii) limitations on small craft carried owing to the need to stow them under davits or handle them by derrick or crane. Many converted ships performed with distinction but they were no substitute for the purpose-built design that emerged as the Landing Ship, Dock, or LSD.

The principle of flooding-down a floating dock, locating a ship inside and raising it clear of the water by pumping out the dock was long established. But to incorporate this system as the after end of an otherwise conventional ship was revolutionary. Detail was kept simple and the first of the *Ashland* class commissioned in 1943, followed by seven sisters in seven months. The layout was a sound one and has survived almost unchanged—except in scale—down to the latest classes of large amphibious ships.

In the early vessels, the docking area was proportionately larger than in more recent designs, being almost 400 feet on an overall length of only 475 feet and giving room for three LCU's. Virtually the whole of the superstructure was built on a bridge spanning the two sides of the dock and running into a conventional ship bow section.

The drawbacks of the design were later evident; they were essentially self-propelled docks, with little space for embarking troops or their material. The rush with which they had to be built meant that their engines were what was available, simple reciprocating units. The disadvantage of these robust prime-movers was their high profile; the docking area ran over the top of engine and boiler rooms, with the large machinery and uptakes thus being sided to prevent their intrusion.

Even while the *Ashlands* were being built, however, the second group was being advanced. With a longer lead-time, low-profile steam turbines could be specified.

Virtually indentical in other respects, this second class, known as the *Casa Grandes,* commissioned from mid-1944 onwards and were planned to be nineteen strong. Small by modern standards, they have a slab-sided appearance conferred by a low bridge atop a long house two decks deep. The funnels, although sided, are not staggered as in later classes, and the two heavy cranes are also opposite each other.

LSD's 17, 18, 20 and 22 have since been modernised and now include a helicopter pad but none now qualifies for the minimum 20-knot requirement and all are in reserve. All the earlier *Ashlands* have disappeared with the exception of the *White Marsh* now serving under the Taiwan flag as the *Tung Hai* and the *Gunston Hall,* with the Argentian Navy as *Candido de Lasala.*

Blue Ridge Amphibious Command Ship   United States

Units: No. LCC 19 (ex-AGC 19) *Blue Ridge*
No. LCC 20 (ex-AGC 20) *Mount Whitney*

	Blue Ridge	*Mount Whitney*
Laid Down:	1967	1969
Launched:	1969	1970
Completed:	1970	1971

Displacement: 19,300 Deep Load
Length (o.a.): 620ft
Beam: 82ft
Draught: 108ft
Machinery: Geared steam turbines 1 shaft 22,000shp for 20 knots
Armament: Two—BPDMS Sea Sparrow SAM launchers
Four—3-inch 50 AA guns
Helicopter: One utility type
Cancelled: AGC 21 (1968)

A modern amphibious landing is a complex affair which demands the proper co-ordination of many separate entities. With land, sea and air forces involved continuous close control is necessary to prevent the whole set-up disintegrating and here, probably more than in any other situation, success will go to the best-equipped force. The need for a specialised command ship was recognised early in the island-hopping war of the Pacific; what was needed then was capacity rather than speed or performance and merchant ship hulls were converted for the job, some, such as the *Mount McKinley* class, giving continuous service since.

The vast armada of war-built landing craft—cumbersome and slow—has now largely disappeared and ideas on amphibious forces revised. One can cater on a permanent basis only for landings on a limited scale and what is maintained in peace-time is only the nucleus which would provide the basis for a rapid expansion on the outbreak of hostilities. Thus, it was possible to lay down one requirement for all amphibious force ships—that they have a minimum sea speed of 20 knots, enabling a force to travel rapidly as a cohesive unit.

The pair of *Blue Ridges* replace in part some of those earlier conversions now being discarded as no longer able to meet requirements. That they resemble *Iwo Jima* class LPH's in profile is no accident as the latter's roomy hull and proven machinery layout was adapted by 'stretching', and built-up topsides to give a unique appearance. A large amount of accommodation is required as the flag and communications staff doubles the ship's basic complement of 700.

The communication systems operated by the attached units have greatly influenced the layout of the upper works as the disposition of the associated antennae has to be such that there is minimum interaction between them.

A rather small mercantile-type bridge structure is set almost amidships on the centre line and is equipped with prominent bridge wings to reach the edge of the hull, which is sponsoned on either side to give maximum deck area. There is no funnel, the uptakes exhausting through angled ducts protruding from the square structure atop the after end of the island.

Forward of the bridge is a prominent lattice mast bearing a horizontal dipole array which is trainable in azimuth. Aft a tapered, square-sectioned tower topped-off with a round platform which bears a ring of what appear to be ECM pods. The flat top of this was designed to take a large search antenna covered by a GRP dome but neither has yet been

No. LCC 19 *Blue Ridge*

fitted. Three smaller light masts bear further communications aerials and there are numerous whips, some of which are adjacent to the helicopter pad aft and are made to swing downwards to clear.

Radar is up to full 'warship' standards with an SPS-48 3D antenna atop the superstructure and an SPS-40 search radar over the bridge. Comprehensive data processing systems are installed to sift the vast mass of incoming information.

Original defensive armament was light, consisting of only four 3-inch 50's mounted forward of the superstructure in positions where their arcs of fire were severely restricted by the ship's cohamper. Two BPDMS Sea Sparrows have now been added abaft the superstructure to compensate.

The use of the sponsons to provide boat stowage is noteworthy.

Mount McKinley Amphibious Command Ship   United States

Units: No. LCC 7 *Mount McKinley* (ex-*Cyclone*)
No. LCC 12 *Estes* (ex-*Morning Star*)
No. LCC 16 *Pocono*
No. LCC 17 *Taconic*

	Mount McKinley	Estes	Pocono	Taconic
Laid Down:	1943	1943	1944	1944
Launched:	1943	1943	1945	1945
Completed:	1944	1944	1945	1946

Displacement: 7,500 standard
12,600 Deep Load
Length (o.a.): 495ft
Beam: 63ft
Draught: 28ft
Machinery: Steam turbine 1 shaft
6,000shp for 16 knots
Armament: One—5-inch DP gun
Four—40mm AA guns (2 × 2)
Aircraft: One helicopter. No hangar
Disposals:

No.	Name	Date
AGC 1	*Appalachian*	1959
AGC 2	*Blue Ridge*	1960
AGC 3	*Rocky Mount*	1960
AGC 5	*Catoctun*	1959
AGC 8	*Mount Olympus*	1961
AGC 9	*Wasatch*	1960
AGC 10	*Auburn*	1960
LCC 11 (ex-AGC 11)	*Eldorado*	1972
AGC 13	*Panamint*	1960
AGC 14	*Teton*	1961
AGC 15	*Adirondack*	1961

This extensive class, originally 15-strong, represented the first attempt to standardise in a single hull the facilities required for the conduct of a large amphibious operation. As accommodation was of greater importance than speed, it was decided to convert suitable merchant ship hulls.

Of the various types then being series produced for the US Maritime Commission, the choice fell on a turbine driven C2. It should be noted that the label 'C2' does not, in itself, define a ship precisely, merely denoting a cargo ship of a certain length. (The well-known *Liberty* and *Victory* classes were also C2's.) This particular class was denoted by C2-S-B11, a modification of the type that became familiar as the backbone of the American merchant marine in the 'fifties, nearly 30 being operated by United States Lines alone.

On completion for their new role, the *Mount McKinleys* differed considerably from their commercial counterparts, with a half-height forecastle and a long bridge deck for extra accommodation space. The majority had a substantial goal-post mast stepped at either end of this deck, although two—*Pocono* and *Taconic*—have a pole mast in the after position. A longer bridge structure was fitted than in the standard merchantman; this was continued full height over its whole length, giving a boxy profile and making the funnel appear shorter. In some, an uptake extension was fitted to obviate down-draught problems.

A tapered, heavy lattice mast topped the bridge and the comprehensive radar fit has been kept well up-dated with the prominent dish of the SPS-30 over the bridge and the rectangular SPS-37 on one of the masts. The TACAN air control pod is also prominent.

Boats were sided at a position abreast of the former Nos 3 and 4 hatches. In spite of all this and various gun-tubs and liferafts, the appearance is still mercantile.

The class was originally classified AGC (Combined Operations Communications HQ and, later, Amphibious Force Flagships) and their highly specialised nature was responsible for the rapid decommissioning of the majority after the war and their subsequent early disposal in 1959-61.

Only five remained, the present quartette and *Eldorado* (AGC 11). These were modernised and re-rated LCC (Amphibious Command Ships).

External changes were small, the most obvious outside the radar fit being the provision of a helicopter pad aft, which meant a reduction in their defensive armament.

They were originally fitted with a single 5-inch 38 gun forward and aft in open tubs, together with four twin 40mm mountings in tubs sided by the forward goal post and right aft. Although half of this armament was removed to provide space for the helicopter pad, there was still not room for a

No. LCC 12 *Estes*

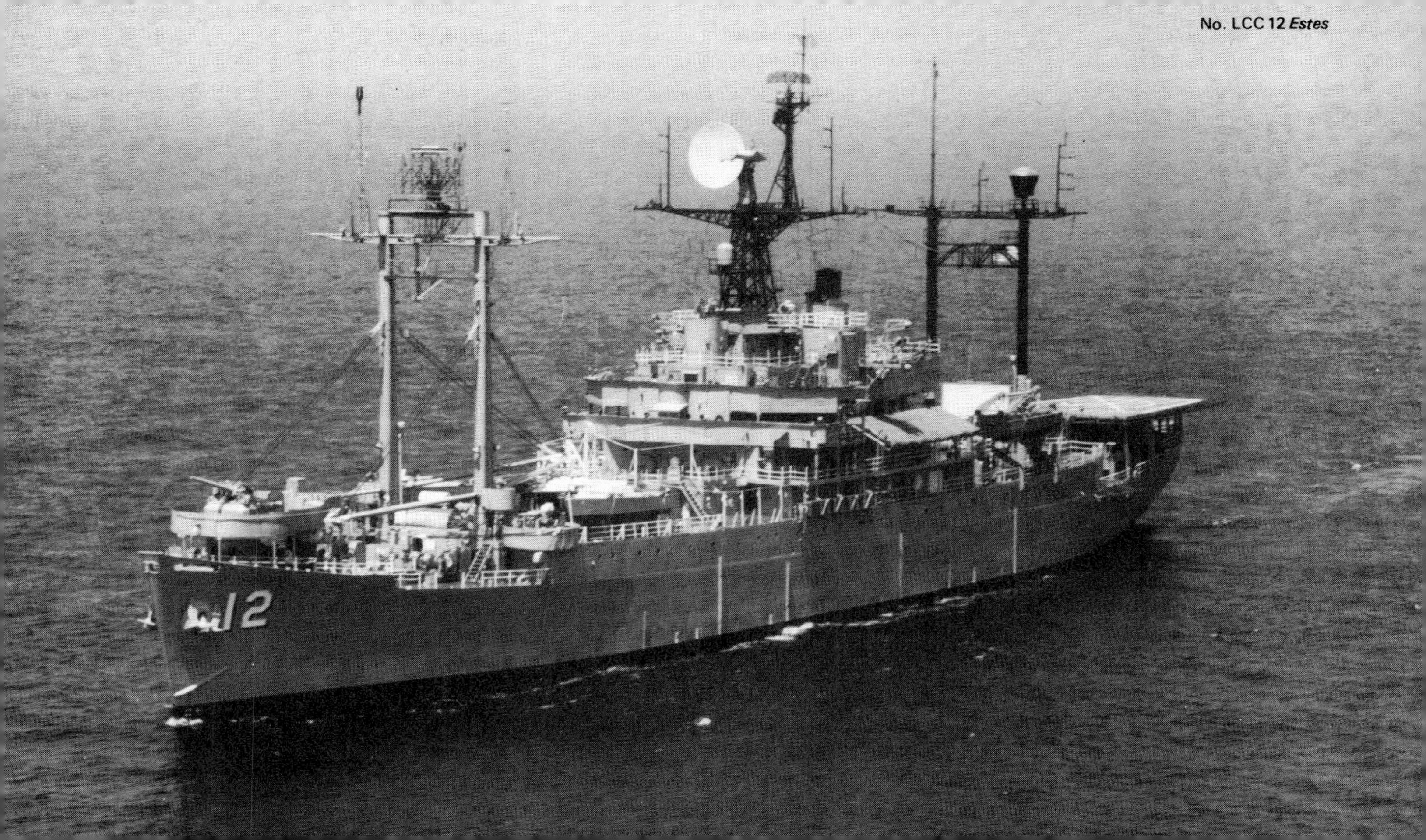

hangar or anything more than minimal facilities.

As with many of the war standards, they have proved to be surprisingly durable and are still probably good for about 15 knots. This is, however, not sufficient for modern requirements and they were withdrawn from service as the *Blue Ridges* commissioned.

Eldorado was disposed of in 1972 and the others are in reserve. Barring emergencies, it is unlikely that they will see further service.

Northampton Command Ship

United States

Units: No. CC1 (ex-CLC1, ex-CA 125) *Northampton*
Laid Down: 1944
Launched: 1951
Completed: 1953
Displacement: 14,700 standard
17,100 Deep Load
Length (o.a.): 676ft
Beam: 71ft
Draught: 29ft
Machinery: Geared steam turbines 4 shafts
120,000shp for 33 knots
Armament: Four—5-inch DP guns (4 × 1)
(only one mounted at present)
Helicopters: Two operated. No hangar

The *Oregon City* class of heavy cruiser was a direct single-funnelled derivative of the extensive *Baltimore* class. They were laid down rather late in World War II and, in spite of fast building times, the three that were eventually completed did not commission until 1946 and, of these, only the much-modified *Albany* remains. Six more were cancelled and work on a seventh, the half complete

Northampton was stopped. It was three years later that work was recommenced on the hull to rebuild it as a Task Fleet Command Ship, graded CLC. The function of this new class of ship was almost identical with the already extant AGC's such as the *Mount McKinleys* but, where these were converted merchantmen of limited speed and self-protection, the ex-cruiser had a speed of about 33 knots, was armoured and able to carry a reasonable defensive armament. She was thus able to form part of a fast carrier task force if necessary and co-ordinate its operations.

The already generous freeboard was increased by the addition of one extra deck to provide extra accommodation, with the superstructure grouped into two compact masses above. Both sections were topped by a large-section tower, bearing massive search antennae.

The dominant feature of the layout was provided by the installation forward of a tapered, unsupported mast 125 feet in height. A shorter mast with a prominent table is placed just forward of the bridge. The wide spread in the positions of the

masts is primarily to avoid interaction between the various antennae that they support.

Armament, from the outset, has been on a rather light scale, with the planned main battery of nine 8-inch guns suppressed in favour of four, single 5-inch 54's in destroyer-type DP mountings and eight 3-inch guns in enclosed twin mountings grouped around the funnel. These were not of the usual type but a 70-calibre weapon similar in length to the British design. The longer range and higher rate of fire of these guns was negated by their unreliable design and they were removed in 1962.

The original layout of the 5-inch armament has also varied from the conventional two forward and two aft configuration. Little more than a token defence, they were normally reduced in number and, latterly, there was only one left, first in 'A' position and then in 'X'. To improve the firing arc of 'A' gun, which was encumbered by the mast on the forecastle, the mounting was offset to starboard of the centreline.

The spacious quarterdeck allows the operation of two helicopters, although there is no covered accommodation for them.

The electronic fit is as complete as would be expected for a ship with such a vital role. A dish antenna of impressive proportions is mounted on the forward tower, replacing the old SPS-2 unit that, at the time, was the largest type in existence. The more familiar SPS-37 search antenna tops the after tower and there are numerous whips and pods for communications, TACAN, ECM and satellite navigation purposes.

The rebuilding of the ship increased her tonnage considerably and her accommodation and communications made her valuable as a flagship. She spent half her life on these duties, being relieved in 1961 for general service and re-rated CC (Command Ship).

She was placed in reserve in 1970 when the new *Blue Ridge* class entered service. These have far superior facilities and *Northampton's* days are probably numbered.

Iowa Battleship

United States

Units: No. BB61 *Iowa*
No. BB62 *New Jersey*
No. BB63 *Missouri*
No. BB64 *Wisconsin*

	Iowa	New Jersey	Missouri	Wisconsin
Laid Down:	1940	1940	1941	1941
Launched:	1942	1942	1944	1943
Completed:	1943	1943	1944	1944

Displacement: 45,500 standard
58,000 Deep Load
Length (o.a.): 887ft
Beam: 108ft
Draught: 38ft
Machinery: Geared steam turbines 4 shafts 212,000shp for 33 knots
Armament: Nine—16-inch guns (3 × 3) Twenty—5-inch guns (10 × 2) A few 40mm (varies. None in *New Jersey*)
Helicopters: Two
Disposals: BB65 *Illinois* LD:45 BU:46 BB66 *Kentucky* LD:44 BU:58

Excepting historically preserved units, the *Iowas* are the world's last surviving battleships. Developed from the *Washington/S. Dakota* type, they were about 6,000 tons heavier than the *Tirpitz* and exceeded in size only by the Japanese *Yamatos*. They were laid down in 1940-1 and completed in about 3 years but by this time the carrier was the more useful type and last two of the planned six were broken up incomplete. The remaining four saw strenuous service in the Pacific, where they acted as support for fast carrier groups, a task now discharged by the modern missile frigate.

Where most of the US Navy's battleships paid off after World War II, the *Iowas* did not decommission until after the Korean War. First to go was *Missouri*, her speed limited after a grounding in 1950. The *Wisconsin* suffered a major fire, affecting her forward turrets.

Useful fire support had been rendered during the Korean War, refining techniques begun in World War II. The Vietnam War offered similar opportunities and *New Jersey*, undamaged and with more up-to-date electronics than *Iowa*, was re-activated in 1967 to attend her third war.

She was fitted with a minimum of modern radars and a very prominent array of ECM antennae. As she was to lay off the coast in a purely fire-support role, the latter were very necessary with her being a potentially attractive target for missiles. Indirect fire support is completely outside the province of a missile armed ship and a recognition of the gun's continuing usefulness is demonstrated in the more powerful conventional armaments now fitted in missile carriers.

The sort of targets worthy of a 16-inch shell of 2,700lb at out to 42,000 yards were lacking, however, and what was probably the last battleship commission ended in December 1969.

The design offered a clean, balanced profile with two triple 16-inch turrets forward and one aft; secondary armament consisted of twenty 5-inch 38's in twin gunhouses. The demands of the Pacific War saw them provided with a large number of smaller automatic weapons; the totals of these

No. BB 62 *New Jersey*

varied from ship to ship, but were typically eighty 40mm and fifty 20mm. By the time they were decommissioned, these had been removed in favour of thirty 3-inch 50's with their better stopping power but these, in turn, have since been removed.

As they were designed to counter ships with a similar armament, their protection was on a massive scale. Vertical side armour was made up to 12 inches thick, with an even heavier area protecting propeller shafts. Turret faces and conning towers had no less than 17 inches.

The aircraft complement was originally of three float planes, housed right aft below the quarterdeck and served by two catapults and a prominent crane. Soon after World War II, the catapults were removed and the aircraft replaced by a pair of helicopters.

The class is over 200 feet longer than the *South Dakotas* from which it stemmed. This is due primarily to the 50 per cent increase in power designed to give them 33 knots, some 3 knots faster than the earlier class. Higher speeds have been attained, helped by the extremely fine hull form which is particularly noticeable forward.

An extended lease of life for these leviathans was promised at one stage by experiments with rocket-assisted, fin-stabilised shells, but these were eventually abandoned in favour of more 'conventional' guided weapons, which could be deployed by much smaller ships.

Canberra Guided Missile Cruiser   United States

Units: No. CA 70 (ex-CA G 2) *Canberra* (ex-*Pittsburgh*)
Laid Down: 1941
Launched: 1943
Completed: 1943
Converted: 1956
Displacement: 13,400 standard
17,800 Deep Load
Length (o.a.): 674ft
Beam: 71ft

Draught: 31ft
Machinery: Geared steam turbines 4 shafts
120,000shp for 33 knots
Armament: Two—twin Terrier SAM launchers
Six—8-inch guns (2 × 3)
Ten—5-inch guns (5 × 2)
Eight—3-inch guns (4 × 2)
Helicopter: Landing space for one. No hangar
Disposal: CA 69 (ex-CA G 1) *Boston* 1973

Originally sister ships of the *Saint Paul* (q.v.), *Canberra* and *Boston* were selected for a pilot conversion project to update the class with the Terrier missile, that had just completed trial firings from the old battleship *Mississippi*. Modifications included a heavily remodelled superstructure, the earlier two funnels giving way to a single, fatter stack that gave them the appearance of *Oregon City* class ships. The after 8-inch turret was removed together with the adjacent 5-inch turrets; smaller automatic weapons were replaced by 3-inch 50's, of which eight still remain. The after superstructure was extended to accommodate two twin launchers and their directors. A heavy lattice foremast was shipped, the mainmast retained in a cut-down form and a platform erected abaft it. The antennae originally mounted during the conversion have since been replaced by more modern gear; currently there is the large SPS-43 mattress atop the mainmast and an SPS-30 dish on the platform.

Although the missiles greatly enhanced the ship's firepower — they were, indeed, the first SAM systems at sea — the conversions were not easy and no more of the class was taken in hand.

The hulls were greatly subdivided and the lines too fine to facilitate the 'open-plan' layout demanded by a missile feed system. Nevertheless, some 150 rounds were shipped in a vertical 'coke-bottle' stowage and feed rates were such that, in theory, the ships could fire 8 Terriers per minute.

On recommissioning, their CA designation was changed to CAG (Guided Missile Heavy Cruiser). Their rebuilding had taken 4 years and they were back in service in 1955/6.

Salem Heavy Cruiser

Units: No. CA 134 *Des Moines*
No. CA 139 *Salem*
No. CA 148 *Newport News*

	Des Moines	Salem	Newport News
Laid Down:	1945	1945	1945
Launched:	1946	1947	1947
Completed:	1948	1949	1949

Displacement: 17,000 standard
21,100 Deep Load
Length (o.a.): 717ft
Beam: 76ft
Draught: 26ft
Machinery: Geared steam turbines 4 shafts 120,000shp for 33 knots
Armament: Nine — 8-inch guns (3 × 3)
Twelve — 5-inch guns (6 × 2)
Twenty — 3-inch guns (10 × 2)
(None in *Newport News*)
Helicopters: Accommodation for two
Cancellations: CA 140 *Dallas*
CA 141-3 } unnamed
CA 149-53 }

The ultimate development of the 8-inch heavy cruiser, this trio came too late to see action in World War II and, like the Russian *Sverdlovs,* seem to be underarmed for their massive size. They

Both ships received various further updatings of a minor nature, mainly electronic, but never received a later version of the Terrier. By 1968, this early model was so limited in comparison with later marks that the ships had their CAG classification reverted to CA (Heavy Cruisers) and were grouped under Fire Support Ships.

With six 8-inch and ten 5-inch guns still remaining, their conventional firepower remained useful, as they proved in bombardment missions during the Vietnam War.

A helicopter pad has been added right aft. It is elevated and offset and for use purely in a utility role as no accommodation is provided and the old aircraft hangar below the quarterdeck cannot be used.

It is of interest that though American cruisers were named after cities (an honour now passed on to fleet nuclear submarines), *Canberra* was the only ever to bear the name of a purely foreign city. The Australian cruiser of this name earned the distinction whilst fighting alongside an American force at the disastrous first battle of Savo Island in 1942.

A year to the day after her completion the American *Canberra* was badly damaged by torpedo whilst engaged in operations against Formosa.

It may be thought that this type of ship, with a heavy gun battery and enhanced AA capability would be useful fleet units but evolution has put more versatile weaponry into smaller hulls which can operate with far smaller crews. Thus, *Boston* was disposed of in 1973 and the *Canberra* which has been in reserve for five years, is not likely to see further active service.

United States

are direct developments of the *Oregon City* class, of which the only survivor is the much-modified *Albany* (q.v.), but they are nearly 50 feet longer. With identical machinery, this extra length can be accounted for only by the new type of fully automatic 8-inch main armament which was fitted. Claimed to have four times the rate of fire of earlier models, this design abandoned separate charges in favour of cased ammunition. The complete round is thus heavy and the automatic handling that much larger to cope with it over a wide range of elevations. Gun barrels are of the same length as previously, with a similar range of about 30,000 yards. Fusing is automatic.

Main battery layout of two triple turrets forward and one aft was virtually standard in American big-gun warships of World War II, being repeated also in battleships and battle cruisers.

The latter type, represented only by the *Alaskas,* carried nine 12-inch guns on a hull only 90 feet longer and it could have been that, had the *Salems* fought in World War II, they would have found themselves out-classed. This paradox was common through faulty appreciation of a design's capabilities. equating size with firepower and an ability to absorb punishment. An example of this type of reasoning pitted battle cruiser against

No. CA 148 *Newport News*

battleship, with results that were repeatedly disastrous.

Twelve of the class were planned, but only three completed.

The appearance of these has changed little over the years and no attempts were made at expensive guided missile conversions. At the time when these hybrids were being rebuilt, the *Salems* were still quite new ships, viable in their own right without missile armament.

As with most American designs, the profile is quite symmetrical with the usual high cruiser freeboard not so noticeable due to the extra length. A fair measure of protection was worked in with side belts up to 8 inches in thickness. The main recognition difference between the *Salems* and the earlier *Oregon City* type lay in the former's very high director towers. These still have their optical range finders and remain a very distinctive feature.

Completion was late enough for the incorporation of twin 3-inch 50's from the outset. There are twenty of these weapons and the class never sported the multiplicity of gun tubs for small automatic weapons common in earlier classes.

The symmetrical layout of the powerful secondary 5-inch armament is also virtually standard in large US cruisers. There are six twin gunhouses, two on the centreline superfiring the main armament and two more on either beam.

Thus it is that three major calibres are mixed in one ship, which seems to have a parallel in pre-*Dreadnought* designs. In the same way that *Dreadnought* herself rationalised armament layout, the guided missile has performed a similar task after the wheel had turned another circle.

The large, characteristically American crane mounted right aft can fold down to deck level. Only *Des Moines* ever had floatplanes and catapults, but these have been removed and all three now carry helicopters.

Only *Newport News* is still in operation, being popular as a flagship. The bridge structure has been built out to the sides of the ship for extra accommodation, and all 3-inch guns removed.

Radar fits are dated, although *Newport News* has an SPS-37 search set and a TACAN pod.

Units: No. CA 73 *St. Paul* (ex-*Rochester*)
Laid Down: 1943
Launched: 1944
Completed: 1945
Displacement: 13,600 standard
17,400 Deep Load
Length (o.a.): 674ft
Beam: 21ft
Draught: 25ft
Machinery: Geared steam turbines 4 shafts
120,000shp for 33 knots
Armament: Nine—8-inch guns (3 × 3)
Ten—5-inch guns (5 × 2)
Twelve—3-inch guns (6 × 2)
Disposals of Baltimore class:
No. CA 68 *Baltimore* 1971
No. CA 69 (ex-CAG 1) *Boston* 1973
No. CA 70 *Canberra* (ex-*Pittsburgh*) see under
'*Canberra*'
No. CA 71 *Quincy* (ex-*St. Paul*) 1973
No. CA 72 *Pittsburgh* (ex-*Albany*) 1973
No. CA 74 *Columbus* now CG 12 see under *Albany*
class
No. CA 75 *Helena* (ex-*Des Moines*) 1974
No. CA 130 *Bremerton* 1973
No. CA 131 *Fall River* 1971
No. CA 132 *Macon* 1969
No. CA 133 *Toledo* 1974
No. CA 135 *Los Angeles* 1974
No. CA 136 *Chicago* now CG 11 see under *Albany*
class

St. Paul is the last conventionally-armed unit of the
Baltimore class although three sisters still exist in
guided missile conversions. Only eight of the class
were originally planned, another six being added
under an emergency war programme. The final
14-strong class was the longest series of heavy
cruisers ever constructed.
Excellent building times were achieved, *Chicago*
for instance taking less than 18 months. The now-
defunct *Oregon City* class were the immediate
derivatives.
The class was little-tried in surface-to-surface
combat, the later war in the Pacific being
dominated by aircraft and the need for shore
support duties. Protection was similar to most
American classes with a waterline belt up to
6 inches thick and horizontal armoured decks of
3 inches and 2 inches to safeguard against
plunging fire and bombs.
The hull has a short protective bulwark right
forward—a very American feature—and a radiused
sheerstrake for added strength. High freeboard is
continued right aft providing space for two
helicopters below the quarterdeck. The aircraft
catapults have long since been removed, although
the prominent crane has been retained. Large
cruisers are popular as flagships, and the extra
small craft associated with these duties are often
stowed abaft the helicopter pad and handled by the
crane.
Overall design stemmed from the *Brooklyns* of
the mid 'thirties (see *General Belgrano*/Argentina).
These were large light cruisers with five triple 6-inch

turrets. The last of the class, *Wichita*, was,
however, completed with three triple 8-inch turrets
on an identical hull. This design having been
proved, it was 'stretched' to become the
Baltimores. The two tall funnels were retained,
prominently capped and the superstructure was
remodelled into a single, corporate mass. Rather
spindly polemasts, which never seemed adequate
to support the increasing complexities of antennae,
were stepped closer to the funnels and raked to
suit. As in British ships of the period, e.g. the
elegant *Dido* class, the aesthetics of raked masts
did not always agree with the mechanical
requirements of rotating aerials and rather unsightly
vertical topmasts were added. In *St. Paul*, a more
substantial tower foremast with lattice topmast has
replaced the original pole.
As completed for the Pacific war, there was the
usual large battery of small, automatic AA
weapons, about fifty 40mm and twenty-four 20mm.
These were subsequently replaced by up to
twenty 3-inch 50's although *St. Paul* carries only
twelve. The other 3-inch guns and the 5-inch
gunhouse abaft 'B' position were taken out when
the ship was modified for flagship duties. The
'midships superstructure was also extended at this
time for extra accommodation.
Whilst serving with the Seventh Fleet during the
Vietnam War, *St. Paul* was used to prove a new
design of rocket-assisted shell, fired from the main
armament. It is not known what sort of accuracies
were achieved, but ranges in excess of 50,000 yards
were claimed. Given time for proper development,
this could have given a new lease of life to the big
gun but it was too late to be more than a token
alternative to the more accurate and harder-hitting
guided missile. As it has proved impracticable to
rebuild cruisers into successful guided missile ships,
the few remaining units are disappearing quickly
and all are due for disposal by 1979.

Ozark Mine Countermeasures Ship
United States

Units: No. MCS 2 (ex-LSV 2, ex-AP 107, ex-CM 7)
Ozark
Laid Down: 1941
Launched: 1942
Completed: 1944
Displacement: 5,900 standard
9,000 Deep Load
Length (o.a.): 455ft
Beam: 60ft
Draught: 20ft
Machinery: Geared steam turbines 2 shafts
11,000shp for 20 knots
Armament: Two — 5-inch DP guns (2 × 1)
Helicopters: Two SH-3 Sea King equivalents
Disposal: *Catskill* (MCS 1) 1970

An unusual example of a warship reversing its designed functions, *Ozark* was ordered under the 1940 programme as one of a group of seven large cruiser-minelayers, classified CM. The nearest equivalent in the Royal Navy was the older *Adventure.*

The extensive mine barrages of World War I were not repeated on a like scale in World War II and the septet were eventually completed to fulfil a variety of functions, only one, the *Terror* (CM 5) actually becoming a full minelayer. Two others, *Catskill* (CM 6) and *Ozark* (CM 7) were re-classified as transports (AP) and then Landing Ships, Vehicle or LSV's, being actually completed in the latter role. The four remaining ships, *Galilea, Monitor, Osage* and *Saugus,* which differed from the others by having only one funnel, were first reclassified Netlayers (AN) and then LSV's also.

All units bore the trademarks of their original calling, a flush-decked, high-freeboard hull, devoid of scuttles over a great part of its length and running aft to a squared-off transom stern. On either side, at main-deck level ran a tunnel along which ran rails which terminated at large doors in the transom. Wheeled dollies ran along these rails bearing the mines, complete with sinkers and cable, to the laying doors.

As LSV's, the ships had these spaces utilised for the stowage of some 40 amphibious tractors or tanks, backed up by about 800 troops. The vehicles could be discharged ashore or directly into the water over a ramp at the after end. This arrangement was unusual and probably not too successful, with the ships being decommissioned very soon after the end of the war.

Although they retained their basic LSV configuration, they were again reclassified in 1956, this time to Mine Warfare Support and Command Ship (MCS), a term which was subsequently refined in stages to Mine Countermeasures Ship.

This all reflected a new type of warfare. Where once all mining, irrespective of depth and other conditions had been by the moored contact variety, shallow water could now be infested with influence mines. These are of three main varieties, magnetic, acoustic or pressure actuated and many highly ingenious variations or combinations of these methods have brought the state of the art to the point where the only sure way to sweep a mine is to detect it and to neutralise it with a counter-charge.

Thus *Ozark* and *Catskill* — actually already decommissioned for disposal in 1961 — were modified

to carry a score of Minesweeping Launches (MSL), to which they acted as support ships. A helicopter pad was added aft, large enough to operate a pair of the RH-3 minesweeping versions of the Sea King. A small mine-laying capability was retained.

Catskill (now MCS 1) was disposed of in 1970 and Ozark, unable to operate the larger RH-53 minesweeping version of the Sea Stallion helicopter, was decommissioned. Although her future seemed very clouded, there have been persistent reports that she may be transferred to Turkey. This makes sense when it is remembered that the Dardanelles/Bosphorus waterway is vital but shallow and vulnerable to mining.

Moskva Helicopter Cruiser   USSR

Units: *Moskva*
Leningrad
Laid Down: 1962-4
Launched: —
Completed: 1967-70
Displacement: 15,000 standard
18,000 Deep Load
Length (o.a.): 645ft
Beam: 76ft
Draught: 25ft
Machinery: Geared steam turbines 2 shafts
100,000shp for 30 knots
Armament: Four—SA-N-3 (Goblet) launchers
(2 × 2)
Two—AS missile launchers (1 × 2)
Four—c. 57mm automatic DP guns (2 × 2)
Two—12-barrelled AS rocket launchers
Helicopters: Twenty

Although the Russians found themselves possessors of an incomplete German aircraft carrier at the end of World War II, they did not complete her and showed little interest in naval air power until a new global policy was given to the Russian Navy. Persistent rumours in the early 'sixties preceded confirmation that a pair of carrier type ships were being built on the Black Sea.

Hybrid ships, they are missile cruisers forward and carrier aft. This arrangement is nothing new and dates back to the days of major semi-conversions such as the Japanese *'Ise'* class. The only really comparable contemporary example is the much smaller French *Jeanne d'Arc* (q.v.).

Described by the Russians as being an AS vessel, she has no arrestor gear, catapults or lifts large enough for conventional aircraft. With her flight deck cut off abruptly by the cliff face of the superstructure, she is clearly geared at present to vertically orientated flight operations, i.e. helicopters. Her dimensions would suggest about 20 Ka-25 Hormones as a practical maximum.

The Russians are, however, developing a V/STOL aircraft—known by the NATO name Freehand—which has already flown from *Moskva* at sea and which could give added punch.

AS functions could well be supplemented by an assault role in a ship of this size. No LCA's are carried and everything would be geared to helicopters. The *Moskvas* compare in size to the American *Iwo Jimas* which, however, are based on

an aircraft carrier design and carry more helicopters in very capacious hulls. They are geared to more specialised operations than the Russian ships, which are designed to operate as part of a task force.

The enormous mast-cum-bridge structure amidships is of a full ship's width. Abaft it is the flight deck which is prominently flared and giving a maximum beam well aft. Access to the elevator is via doors in the after end of the superstructure.

The sheer after end of the bridge profile falls in a series of distinctive steps forward, giving levels for the two twin SA-N-3 Goblet launchers and their directors. There are the usual two 12-barrelled AS rocket launchers on the forecastle. Abaft these is what appears at first sight to be another SAM launcher but is in reality a prototype AS weapon. As it has not been fitted subsequently to other classes, it may well have been less than successful, particularly in view of the possible AS potential of the SS-N-10.

The prominent 3-D radar antennae show an ability to co-ordinate operations sharing data with similar equipped ships.

Twin 57mm gun turrets flank the bridge structure.

So far as anything can be read into Russian nomenclature, it would be expected that prestigious names like *Moskva* and *Leningrad* would be borne by the largest ships of the fleet but, after only the two were completed the design was superseded by a larger class, the *Kurils* (q.v.). It is possible that they proved too modest in size to operate the next generation of aircraft of a fleet that is becoming ever more wide-ranging in its activities.

Kuril Aircraft Carrier USSR

Units: *Kiev*
Minsk
(plus one more reported under construction)

	Kiev	*Minsk*
Laid Down:	1970	1974-5
Launched:	—	—
Completed:	1975	—

Displacement: c. 40,000
Length (o.a.): 925ft
Beam: 200ft (over flight deck)
Machinery: Probably steam turbines
Armament: Four—SA-N-3 (Goblet) launchers (2 × 2)
Six—SA-N-4 launchers (3 × 2)
Two—AS missile launchers (1 × 2)
Two—12-barrelled AS rocket launchers
Twenty-eight—57mm automatic DP guns (14 × 2)
Aircraft: 20 + V/STOL fighters
20 + Helicopters

At a time when the large carrier is really in its last phase of development in the West due to its cost and vulnerability, the Russians have come up with one of their occasional surprise moves and have two under construction. With no previous experience outside the *Moskvas*—only half the size—they are bold indeed to proceed with two that are directly comparable in size with Britain's *Ark Royal*.

The design concept is, however, very different due to the Russian Navy's operating functions. The prime reason for the Royal Navy is the defence of the trade essential to life in the UK. It is, therefore, primarily an escort fleet. The vastness of the USSR is virtually self-supporting. Its merchant fleet operates for the benefit of the State but is not

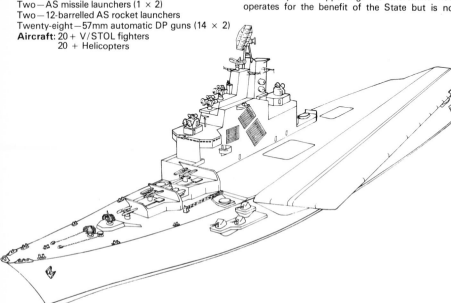

essential for its survival. The Soviet fleet, therefore, is an instrument for demonstrating and, if necessary, delivering power. As the West has created power vacuums in withdrawing its main naval presence from such areas as the Indian Ocean and the Mediterranean, the Russians have discovered the advantages accruing to the latent strength of a flag-showing warship. Their forces are moving ever farther afield and, with few permanent forward bases, range and self sufficiency are important. These are partly a function of size and potential units for a long-range task group are already at sea—the *Kara* and *Krivak* classes are well fitted for complementing the *Kuril* at the centre of a force.

With their great operating experience in submarine nuclear plant, the Russian Navy's next stage may well be the evaluation of this system in surface ships.

Politically the ship is described as an 'anti-submarine cruiser'; a title as meaningless as that of the British 'through deck cruiser'. With a profile very much like a scaled-up *Moskva,* she is very different in having the superstructure offset to starboard. An angled flight deck lays to port of it, extending as far forward as the bridge front. Forward of this, it is blocked-off by the missile mounting decks on the centre line.

The hangar space under the 600-foot flight deck is sufficient to house over 20 of the trusty *Hormone* or the new *Hind* derivative helicopter. In addition, however, is space for the same number of V/STOL fighters such as Freehand which will benefit from the short take-off dimensions of the flight deck. No catapults or arrestor gear are known to have been fitted, allowing no operation of fixed wing 'conventional' aircraft.

Missile disposition of two twin SA-N-3 (Goblet) SAM and one twin AS launcher is much the same as that of the *Moskvas* but, in addition, up to three of the unobtrusive SA-N-4 silo mounted launchers may be incorporated in the weapon fit.

Rather surprisingly, a heavy conventional armament of fourteen twin 57mm gun mountings is grouped aft and forward of 'midships.

Radar and apparent ECM establishment conforms to the usual major warship scale.

Kynda Guided Missile Destroyer

USSR

Units: *Admiral Fokin*
Admiral Golovko
Groznyi
Varyag
Laid Down: 1960-1
Launched: 1961-2
Completed: 1962-5
Displacement: 4,750 standard
6,000 Deep Load
Length (o.a.): 840ft
Beam: 51ft
Draught: 17ft
Machinery: Two sets geared steam turbines 2 shafts
100,000shp for 35 knots
Armament: Eight—SS-N-3 Shaddock launchers (2 × 4)
Two—SA-N-1 Goa launchers (1 × 2)
Four—3-inch (76mm) automatic DP guns (2 × 2)
Two—12-barrelled AS rocket launchers
Six—21-inch AS TTS (2 × 3)

Immediately pre-dating the *Kashins* was the quartette of *Kyndas.* They are of similar dimensions but of greatly different appearance and function and they would appear to be an anti-surface escort complementary to the AA orientated *Kashins.*

The design incorporates steam turbines and the restricted number in the class suggests the uncertainty of design direction at the time.

The anti-surface punch carried is formidable but cumbersome, being centred around two quadruple SS-N-3 Shaddock launchers. These, looking like banks of overgrown torpedo tubes, are placed forward and aft and fire a hefty 40-foot missile with a useful range in excess of 100 miles. Shaddocks however, are not self-homing over their complete trajectory and require a mid-course correction when deployed against over-the-horizon targets.

The agency for this correction is normally airborne and the puzzling omission on this class is the helicopter which would be the obvious solution. Although a pad is marked out on the quarterdeck, no hangar or facilities are provided, so that a *Kynda* would need to work in conjunction with another unit or aircraft in order to realise her full potential.

The forward launcher backs on to the featureless lower deck of the bridge structure and the after one on to the quarterdeck hance. This would suggest that at least one spare round per tube is carried, although the size and weight of the missile would preclude more.

Primary AA defence rests on a twin SA-N-1 Goa launcher mounted forward on what seems to be a very exposed site from the point of view of icing in particular.

The radars for search and control have been the primary factors influencing the layout of the tophamper which is on a massive scale, rather topheavy in appearance.

This has been aggravated by a belt-and-braces approach with all major systems doubled-up. Most of the antennae are housed on the two squaresectioned tower masts of distinctly unlovely aspect. An early 'Head Net' search radar crowns each. 'Scoop Pairs' protrude fore and aft to control the Shaddocks whilst a 'Peel Group' director is atop the bridge to guide the Goa. This doubling reflects the necessary self-reliance of each vessel of a navy that has few permanent foreign bases for support.

Right forward, in a position offering good firing arcs but little protection are two twelve-barrelled AS rocket launchers. Close-in AS protection is afforded by a triple bank of torpedo tubes on either

Varyag

side of the break in the superstructure amidships, connected by rails along the deck to a single handling space.

With no helicopter or VDS, AS information is dependent entirely upon hull-mounted sonar.

Two twin automatic 76mm DP gun turrets are mounted aft with direction from the 'Owl Screech' disc abaft the after funnel.

An interesting feature is the adherence to scuttles in the hull, indicating a limited ability to shut-down in the event of nuclear fall-out but offering fresher living conditions below.

Kashin Guided Missile Destroyer USSR

Units: *Komsomolyets Latvyi*
Komsomolyets Ukranyi
Krasny Kavkaz
Krasny Krim
Obraztsovyi
Odrennyi
Ognevoi
Otlikhnyi
Otvazhnyi
Provedennyi
Provornyi
Sdergiannyi
Slavnyi
Smelyi
Smetlinyi
Soobrazitelvyi
Sposobnyi
Steregushchyi
Strognyi
Stroynyi
Laid Down: 1960-3
Launched: —
Completed: 1962-5
Displacement: 4,300 standard
5,200 Deep Load
Length (o.a.): 475ft
Beam: 52ft
Draught: 19ft

Machinery: 8 sets of gas turbines 2 shafts
96,000shp for 35 knots
Armament: Four—3-inch (76mm) (2 × 2)
Two—twin SA-N-1 (Goa) missile launchers
Two—12-barrelled ASW rocket launchers
Two—6-barrelled ASW rocket launchers
Five—21-inch TT (ASW) (1 × 5)

A class rated as destroyers, the *Kashins* illustrate the difficulty in categorising the modern warship, where even frigates can exceed the tonnages of earlier light cruisers and deploy many times their striking power.

Appearing first in 1962 they were noteworthy as being the first major warships in the world to rely solely on gas turbine propulsion. This was six years before the British commissioned the ex-Type 14 *Exmouth* as a trials ship for similar systems.

Confidence in the design was evident in the unusually large number in the class. Great advantages lie in using the gas turbine, which is looked upon as a replaceable item. Normally, having completed its designated number of running hours, it is removed for overhaul and exchanged. Faulty units are also replaced rather than repaired 'in house', an operation which is well within the capabilities of a depot ship and taking as little as six hours to complete. Gas turbines are very compact

nd self-contained but very inefficient when run
much below their designed rating—thus the
'ashins have eight sets on two propeller shafts,
nabling them to shut down units completely for
ow speed work and thus run the remainder at
ormal rating. This arrangement is very flexible
when associated with variable pitch propellers.

Power boost and ship acceleration is rapid with
ew problems involved in starting from cold. The
ystem lends itself well to automation and consequent reduction in crew numbers.

Outward evidence of gas turbines lies in the two
eed pairs of large funnels, the after pair set right
ack above a more confined section of the hull and

illustrating again the compactness of this form of
propulsion.

This vee configuration is necessary to lead
corrosive gases clear of the tophamper.

Hull profile is typical of Soviet ships, with a long
sweeping sheerline and heavily raked bow with a
characteristic knuckle running almost the full
length.

The class is equipped primarily for an AA role
with an SA-N-1 Goa twin launcher in 'B' and 'X'
positions. This is a rather dated and marinised army
SAM missile with a range of about 15 miles. Both
launchers are mounted atop low magazine
structures; control is by the distinctive 'Peel Group'

directors on the bridge and on a tower forward of the after uptakes.

Several types of search radar antennae are deployed by the class dependent upon degrees of updating.

There are no anti-surface missiles, defence being vested in two twin 76mm automatic gun mountings, radar laid by the two dish antennae of the 'Owl Screech' systems.

AS armament is conventional but fairly powerful. Two twelve-barrelled AS rocket launchers flank the bridge and two six-barrelled units are sided by the after radar tower. A quintuple AS torpedo tube bank is mounted quite high amidships.

Directions for these, however, must be only from hull mounted sonar. No VDS is fitted and, althoug a pad is marked out on the quarterdeck for helicopter, none is usually carried and no backu facilities are provided.

Names and pennant numbers are uncertain an are changed from time to time.

In 1975, at least *Ognevoi* and *Sdergiannyi* wei observed to be up-dated, with four SS-N-1 launchers. Two of these were either side of th after funnel casing. Four multi-barrelled 30m guns were fitted in addition. This heavy augmen tation of the armament has necessitated a ten-fo section to be inserted in the hull. This modernis ation will probably be applied to the whole class.

Kresta I Guided Missile Cruiser

Units: *Admiral Drozd*
Admiral Zozulya
Sevastopol
Vladivostok
Laid Down: 1964-7
Launched: 1965-8
Completed: 1967-9
6,500 Deep Load
Displacement: 5,100 standard
Length (o.a.): 510ft
Beam: 55ft
Draught: 18ft
Machinery: Steam turbines 2 shafts
100,000shp for 33.5 knots
Armament: Four — SS-N-3 Shaddock launchers (2 × 2)
Four — SA-N-1 Goa launchers (2 × 2)
Four — 57mm automatic DP guns (2 × 2)
Two — 12-barrelled rocket launchers
Two — 6-barrelled rocket launchers
Ten — 21-inch AS TT (2 × 5)

Based on lengthened *Kynda* hull, this small class appeared first in 1967. Whereas the *Kyndas* have a massive SSM armament, the *Kresta I's* show a newer and more realistic line of thought in suppressing one of the SS-N-3 Shaddock mountings in favour of another SA-N-1 Goa launcher. The ship is thus better equipped to survive in such areas of sea as the Baltic, where enemy air activity would be intense.

The sheer size of the quadruple Shaddock bank presented many problems to the designers and they have here been split into two pairs and mounted much lower on either side of the bridge where surprisingly, they can be not only elevated considerably but trained out on to the beam, lessening gathering problems without needing to turn the ship.

By suppressing the after launcher, the associated radars and directors are, of course, made redundant and the massive tophamper of the *Kyndas* has been very much reduced. With adequate stability an ever-constant problem in heavily armed ships of this size, a reduction in superstructure is a bonus worth winning.

The Shaddock mountings' forward ends butt up to a low deckhouse built to the sides of the hu and so large that it gives the appearance of forecastle deck and hance. It is really a magazine built topsides in a position unthinkable in conventional gun-armed ship. A probable tw reloads per tube are housed within, with othe space devoted to the missiles for the forwai SA-N-1 Goa launcher mounted on top. A secon launcher is mounted aft and the directors fi these — the rather bizarre so-called 'Peel Groups' - stand isolated on the low bridge and afte superstructure. This latter construction is flanke by compact automatic twin 57mm gun turrets. A the expense of its firing arcs, the convention armament has thus been moved forward, vacatin enough room aft for a hangar to be built at th forward end of the quarterdeck, a space marke out to operate a Ka-25 Hormone helicopter.

This is a very valuable addition to the shir allowing the independent control over the SSM' out to their optimum range of possibly 200 miles. secondary duty of the 'chopper' is in an AS role allowing detection and attack out to a far greate range than that possible by the ship which neve theless carries two twelve-barrelled AS rocke launchers firing forward and two six-barrelle units flanking the hangar aft. These are backed u by quintuple banks of 21-inch AS torpedo tube sided in the waist.

The ship is dominated by the strange 'midship structure, separate from the bridge. The forwar side elongates into a pyramidal radar tower bearin search radar, control radar for the SSM's and ECN pods. The after end is really a pair of athwartshi funnels in a single casing and with exits canted t take fumes clear of the air surveillance antenn mounted above. This funnel arrangement earlier le to the belief that the class was gas turbin propelled.

Kresta II Guided Missile Cruiser

Units: *Admiral Isakov*
Admiral Makarov
Admiral Nakhimov
Admiral Oktyabrskyi
Marshal Voroshilov
Kronstadt
Laid Down: 1968-
Launched: —
Completed: 1972-
Displacement: 6,000 standard
7,500 Deep Load
Length (o.a.): 520ft
Beam: 55ft
Draught: 20ft
Machinery: Steam turbines 2 shafts
100,000shp for 33.5 knots
Armament: Eight—SS-N-10 launchers (2 × 4)
Four—SA-N-3 Goblet launchers (2 × 2)
Four—57mm automatic DP guns (2 × 2)
Two—12-barrelled rocket launchers
Two—6-barrelled rocket launchers
Ten—21-inch AS TT (2 × 5)

The *Kresta I* programme was terminated at four units owing to the availability of two new weapon systems more in keeping with a new line in tactical thought.

The basic hull was retained, though stretched by some 10 feet and the steam turbine kept in preference to the gas turbine. The resultant design on what is still a modest displacement, can only be regarded as a formidable fighting machine which is capable of engaging aerial, surface or submarine targets with equally powerful weaponry. The major weapon shipped is the SS-N-10 SSM first seen on the *Krivaks.*

In place of the two hundred mile nuclear warhead capability of the older Shaddock of the *Kresta I's,* we now have a smaller missile of only horizon range, which can be controlled all the way by the launch ship without recourse to the helicopter that she carries. There is a strong possibility that the SS-N-10 has a limited AS capability in addition.

It is probably a derivative of the proven Styx SS-N-2A fitted in the *Osa* and *Komar* class fast attack craft and its smaller dimensions have allowed the fitting of eight launch tubes. As with the earlier class they are sided at the bridge, but the mounts are quadruple with the launchers in square configuration.

Again, the low deckhouse type magazines are a feature. Again they have SAM launchers on top, but these are now for the SA-N-3 Goblet, a longer-ranged (20 miles) improvement of the Goa. A new-style director is mounted in the same position as before. It now has a superimposed system appropriately called 'Head Light'.

The 'midships structure is broadly similar to that on the earlier class but the 'Head Net' search radar antenna has now been given the hot spot atop the split funnel, yielding pride-of-place to an enormous scanner called 'Top Sail' which gives 3-D data to the action information centre and probably supplemented by helicopter-borne radar. Thi continuous flow of data is computer-assessed an each target allocated an appropriate missile in th order of the threat posed by it.

The helicopter now operates from a flying dec raised one level above the low fantail, a space liabl to become untenable in a large sea.

The bows have gained a sharp, aggressive rak with anchors set right forward to drop them clear o what must be a sonar dome of magnificen proportions beneath.

This and helicopter borne sonar pass informatio on submerged targets to rocket launchers an torpedo tubes mounted similarly to those on the *Kresta I's.*

Two 57mm turrets are similarly disposed, but ar interesting addition are eight 30mm guns ir twinned automatic turrets amidships. Their role is uncertain but could possibly be similar to that of the American Vulcan/Phalanx as a 'last-ditch' anti-mis sile armament.

Krivak Guided Missile Destroyer

Units: *Bditelnyi*
Bodryi
Doblestnyi
Dostroynyi
Silnyi
Storozhevoy
Svirepyi
Laid Down: 1968-
Launched: —
Completed: 1971-
Displacement: 3,800 standard
4,900 Deep Load
Length (o.a.): —
Beam: 50ft
Draught: 16ft
Machinery: 8 sets gas turbines 2 shafts
110,000shp for 37 knots
Armament: Four—3-inch (76mm) (2 × 2)
Four—SS-N-10 SSM launchers (1 × 4)
Two—SA-N-4 SAM launchers (2 × 1)
Two—12-barrelled AS rocket launchers
Eight—21-inch AS TT (2 × 4)

First appearing in 1971, the *Krivaks* may be regarded as replacements for the *Kashins* and it is interesting to see the changes in design resulting from a near decade of experience.

Although considerably shorter, the newer ships are still comparable in tonnage but, with a sleek uncluttered profile, they appear to be considerably smaller particularly in less-than-perfect visibility.

The eight sets of gas turbines have been retained

but their layout has obviously been greatly improved with their uptakes now grouped into a single square funnel, large and squat and barely recognisable as such.

More advanced and compact radar arrangements topside have combined to make possible a good 'single ended' layout.

The most notable improvement is in the missile armament which is formidable indeed. The *Kashins'* lack of an SSM has been rectified by the quadruple SS-N-10 launcher forward. The missile associated with these is of about 30 miles range compared with the 100 plus of the older SS-N-3 Shaddock that it appears to replace. The overall smaller ranges of newer missilry are an interesting comment on changes of thinking and control difficulties experienced with long range non-self-homing hardware.

The N-10's are controlled by the twin 'Head Light' directors above the bridge with overall search and surveillance by the 'Head Net' antenna atop the mast. The light lattice mast hung on the back of the main structure is reminiscent of Japanese practices.

Two SA-N-4 SAM systems are also incorporated. These are retractable in silos and are easily overlooked with their low profile when housed. One is situated immediately abaft the SSM launchers forward and the other abaft the funnel. These missiles have a near 20-mile range.

Information for AS operations is from a bow mounted sonar (indicated by the pronounced rake

to take anchors clear) and a VDS aft. No helicopter is carried, indicating a confidence in doing without it rather than an oversight, i.e. the N-10 probably has some AS capability.

Medium range AS punch is given by two twelve-barrelled rocket launchers firing over fairly wide arcs from a position forward of the bridge. These are backed up for shorter range by two quadruple banks of AS torpedo tubes sided abaft the bridge.

The hull does not have the rather exaggerated sheer of earlier classes and drops one level to the quarterdeck. This makes easier and neater the superimposed layout of the two automatic twin 76mm DP turrets, whose director is situated immediately forward of the funnel.

The design appears to offer a very successful package on a reasonable tonnage and an extended series is likely with some seven already commissioned and others under construction. In addition, they continue the distinctive 'made in Russia' appearance which is common to all new classes and indicating a sound continuity of design.

Kara Guided Missile Cruiser $\qquad$ USSR

Units: *Nikolaev*
Ochakov
+1
Completed: 1972-
Displacement: 10,000 standard
Length (o.a.): 560ft
Beam: 62ft
Draught: 20ft
Machinery: Gas turbines on twin shafts
Armament: Eight—SS-N-10 launchers (2 × 4)
Four—SA-N-3 (Goblet) launchers (2 × 2)
Two—SA-N-4 launchers (2 × 1)
Two—12-barrelled AS rocket launchers
Two—6-barrelled AS rocket launchers
Ten—21-inch AS TT (2 × 5)

The *Kresta II* class probably represented the maximum amount of hardware that could be fitted inside a hull of limited dimensions, although each preceding type had shown an enlargement. Modern threats to a warship are constantly changing and Russian practice is to counter each and every one in the same hull. As it was thought desirable to counter the close-range aerial threat more adequately, the next type had to be increased in size quite substantially if the offensive capabilities were not to suffer.

Thus, the *Kresta* hull was again stretched, this time by 10%, resulting in a ship approaching 10,000 tons displacement. There exists a close similarity with the earlier classes, recalling the confusing likeness between German major warships of World War II.

Layout is very similar to that of the *Kresta II* but the extra length has resulted in a slightly less cluttered appearance.

From the recognition aspect, the practical differences lie in a 'foremast' and a more obvious

Nikolaev

funnel of clean lines and without an antenna atop.

The SS-10 SSM is again the primary weapon, quadrupled under either bridge wing and possibly reloaded from similar extensive deckhouse magazines.

SA-N-3 Goblet SAM launchers are in the same positions atop the deckhouses, loading vertically through small hatches laying adjacent. These missiles are controlled by the massive 'Head Light' directors prominent at either end of the 'midships structures. They are double-dished units capable of both tracking the target and guiding the missile over its full time of flight.

Amidships lies the bonus gained from the extra hull length. Firstly, inconspicuous silos on either side of the mast house the SA-N-4 (used also in the *Krivaks* and tested on *Sverdlov* conversions). As it has a similar range to the N-3, the difference presumably lies in its operating altitude. Probably a near relation to the land-based *Strela* missile the N-4 could be a potent answer to enemy helicopters and low flying aircraft, with reaction times possibly quick enough to counter an incoming low-level missile.

Backing up the N-4 is an enhanced 'conventional' fit. Twin 76mm gun turrets have reappeared in the waist, replacing the briefly used 57mm of earlier classes. They are controlled by the 'Owl Screech' dishes on the bridge wings.

Four automatic 30mm cannon flank the funnel casing with adjacent 'Drum Tilt' directors. These are almost certainly multi-feed developments of the *Kresta's* weapons with parallels in the American C.I.W.S.

AS weaponry is on a similar scale and has the same disposition as in the earlier classes. The helicopter hangar opens on to a flight deck elevated above the quarterdeck, on which is mounted a VDS installation.

The massive funnel with adjacent back-facing air intakes betrays gas turbine propulsion. A similar machinery fit to the *Krivaks* would give this very clean-lined vessel a speed of about 32 knots.

The truly incredible range of systems carried by the *Karas* would result in expenditure that must surely limit their numbers.

Kirov Light Cruiser   USSR

Units: *Kirov*
Slava

	Kirov	Slava
Laid Down:	1935	1936
Launched:	1936	1939
Completed:	1938	1944

Displacement: 8,600 standard
11,000 Deep Load
Length (o.a.): 627ft
Beam: 58ft
Draught: 20.5ft
Machinery: Geared steam turbines with cruising diesels 2 shafts
112,000shp for 34.5 knots
Armament: Nine—7.1-inch (180mm) (3 × 3)
Six—3.9-inch (100mm) (6 × 1)
Eight—37mm
Space for six 21-inch TT
Sixty to ninety mines
Discarded: *Maksim Gorki*
Kaganovitch
Kalinin
Voroshilov
Destroyed on stocks: *Ordzhonikidze*

Only two units now remain of this, the first class of cruiser to be built in the USSR since the Revolution. They were planned in the era when the cruiser designs of the great naval powers were being tailored to the strictures imposed by the Washington Treaty of 1922 and, as insufficient design expertise was then available within the Soviet Union, assistance was sought from the Genoa firm of Ansaldo.

Italian treaty designs favoured a reasonable armament and an exceptionally high speed. As the displacement was limited, these requirements were realised at the expense of hull weight. Some protection was usually worked in, so the hull proper tended to be of very light construction. Bunker space was severely restricted, but the Italian sphere of interest was largely Mediterranean and lack of range of little account.

The resultant ship was handsome, of well balanced profile and closely akin to contemporary Italian Fleet units.

Main armament was wisely restricted to 180mm (7.1-inch) rather than the 8-inch maximum stipulated by the treaty and nine of these weapons were mounted in three triple turrets. These are somewhat inhibiting in that each group of three guns is mounted in a common sleeve, necessitating that they all elevate together.

The earlier secondary armament consisted of eight 4-inch DP guns, but these have been replaced by six 3.9-inch in single mountings on a gundeck around the after funnel and well laid out for practice drill.

Range was enhanced by the inclusion of diesels which can be clutched into the two main shafts for cruising. The high speed of over 34 knots was provided by geared steam turbines with their necessarily higher fuel consumption. Light armour protection is worked in around sides, deck and gunhouses.

Russian naval policy at the time was geared to its own shallow water approaches and the mine was of great importance. This is reflected in the *Kirovs* having deck-mounted mine rails with a capacity of over 100 and discharging over the quarters.

Although they have had postwar modifications—including the removal of the aircraft catapult and installation of improved Search and Fire Control Radars—they are now obsolete and

Kirov

used for training, a function outwardly visible in the large deckhouse forward of 'Y' turret.

Recognition is easiest by the bridge structure detail, *Kirov* having her director atop a heavy tripod with the *Slava* having hers on a tower, with a light tripod mast behind. *Slava* was, earlier, named *Molotov*, the change of name being doctrinal.

Six of the class were eventually completed, a further one having been destroyed on the stocks to prevent capture in 1941. Others had been planned.

Chapaev Light Cruiser

USSR

Units: *Komsomolets* (ex-*Chkalov*)
Zheleznyakov
Laid Down: 1939/40
Launched: 1941/47
Completed: 1948/50
Displacement: 11,500 standard
15,000 Deep Load
Length (o.a.): 659ft
Beam: 63ft
Draught: 24ft
Machinery: Geared steam turbines with cruising diesels 2 shafts
115,000shp for 34 knots
Armament: Twelve—6-inch (152mm) (4 × 3)
Eight—3.9-inch (100mm) (4 × 2)
100-200 mines
Discarded: *Chapeav*
Frunze
Kuibyshev

The limitations of the *Kirovs* imposed by ceiling on displacement and by the old-fashioned 7.1-inch gun armament were evident before they were even completed. Thus, before any experience of the class could be 'ploughed-back', another, enlarged version was commenced.

By the latter 'thirties, few of the Washington Treaty limitations were still being adhered to and the new class was of 50% greater displacement on a hull about 40 feet longer. By reducing the gun calibre to 152mm (6-inch), four triple turrets could be accommodated. Each gun could also now elevate independently.

The haste with which this class was begun was probably due to the imminence of war. They were too late, however, and of the six planned, the five finally completed did not commission until well after cessation of hostilities.

In appearance, they are very similar to the *Kirovs,* but can be identified by their four turrets and vertical funnels, with an additional gun director prominent aft.

As before, cruising diesels have been incorporated for economy. This complicated the engine and boiler room layout and resulted in the widely spaced uptakes that give the characteristic silhouette.

This class boasts eight 3.9-inch guns as the secondary armament, disposed British-style in four twin mountings around the after funnel. Lighter 37mm weapons are twinned around the bridge and after superstructure in groups.

Mine capacity was extended by about one-eighth, with the deck launching rails extending on either side from the counter to well forward of X-turret.

Although completed postwar, some of the class were equipped with aircraft catapults and torpedo tubes. These were removed during modifications during the 'fifties. A decade later saw a modernising refit during the course of which modern search and gunnery radars were fitted. Wisely, no expensive attempts were made to add missiles to the weapon fit.

The robust simplicity of a proven gun system has much to commend it in reliability terms when compared with the delicacy of the electronics of more advanced controls, particularly when far from base resources.

The primary obvious influence on the class is Italian, but echoes remain of the German technical help rendered to the Russian Navy prior to 1941. The secondary gun directors at the break of the forecastle are almost indentical with the familiar German *'Wackeltöpfe'* of World War II.

Three of the class have been discarded and the remaining pair can only be regarded as obsolete, although their roomy accommodation (by modern standards) gives them a useful lease of life as training ships.

It should be noted that, with all Soviet warships, little credence should be placed on pennant numbers for recognition purposes. They are often changed when a ship is transferred between fleets.

Komsomolets

Sverdlov Light Cruiser

USSR

Units: *Admiral Lazarev*
Admiral Senyavin
Admiral Ushakov
Aleksandr Nevsky
Aleksandr Suvorov
Dimitri Pozharski
Dzerzhinski
Mikhail Kutusov
Murmansk
Oktiabrskaia Revoluitsiia
Sverdlov
Zhdanov
Laid Down: 1948-53
Launched: 1951-4
Completed: 1952-8
Displacement: 15,000 standard
19,000 Deep Load
Length (o.a.): 689ft
Beam: 72ft
Draught: 24.5ft
Machinery: Geared steam turbines 2 shafts
140,000shp for 34 knots
Armament: Twelve—6-inch (152mm) (4 × 3)
Twelve—3.9-inch (100mm) (6 × 2)
Ten—21-inch TT discarded
About 200 mines
Discarded: *Admiral Nakhimov*
Scrapped: *Ordzhonikidze*

The *Sverdlovs* continued the direct line of development in Soviet cruiser construction, being laid down whilst the *Chapaevs* were still completing in the late 'forties. They are about 30 feet longer than the preceding class and closely follow them in layout. In profile, they present a more solid, built-up appearance with the forecastle deck taken right back to a point just forward of X-turret, giving a more sea-kindly hull for northern conditions. Abeam of the forefunnel the deck rises one level higher for a short distance.

The classification of 'light cruiser' is based solely on the 152mm (6-inch) main battery and seems a little pale for ships of this size, whose only real foreign equivalent were the pair of American *Worcesters*.

They could well have mounted a heavier calibre weapon and the adherance to this earlier gun reflects the lack of innovation at this time and a continued dependence on established German designs.

They are, nevertheless, formidable ships by conventional standards and could have posed problems if used as commerce raiders. This may not have been their main intended rôle, however, as the cruising diesels of the earlier classes have been omitted. Range is still quite considerable.

A twin-shaft layout is still favoured, making for a cheaper and simpler hull design.

Some 24 units were planned for the class but postwar shortages slowed down this rather ambitious total and naval thinking overtook them in as much as the large cruiser as a type was now considered passé. 17 of the class progressed to the launching stage, but only 14 were finally completed, all by 1956.

The first to commission was the name ship *Sverdlov*, which made a well timed debut at the British Coronation Review of 1953.

Completing some years after similar units in the West, they became very much 'ideas looking for an application'. Their superfluity was underlined by the premature transfer of the *Ordzhonikidze* to Indonesia in 1962. Renamed *Irian*, she proved a technological embarrassment to the severely limited resources of her new owners and was allowed to run down and was eventually scrapped. Similar plans for a presentation to the UAR not surprisingly fell through.

In spite of the relatively light armament, final tonnage exceeded design figures by about 2,000 tons, partly accounted for by the armour protection, which was up to about 5 inches in hull belts and gunhouses.

There has been little attempt to convert the class to missile armament. *Dzerzhinski* emerged in the early 'sixties with a prototype twin SA-N-1 Guideline SAM launcher in place of X-turret. Radar-guided out to about 20 miles, this big missile was a marinised version of an army weapon. It was not a success and has not been repeated, giving way to the more effective SA-N-1 Goa.

Zhdanov also lost her X-turret, in this case to the recent SA-N-4, a compact silo-mounted weapon with a 20-mile range which is probably here being evaluated.

Admiral Senyavin is somewhat similar with a large deckhouse and extra mast but has lost both main after turrets and can now operate a Ka-25 Hormone helicopter.

Sverdlov

Pennant Numbers of Subject Ships

Note: *1 Characters in parentheses do not appear*
on the ship
2 Numbers of Russian ships are not in-
cluded owing to their frequent changes

(CC)	1	*Northampton*
(LHA)	1	*Tarawa*
(LPD)	1	*Raleigh*
(PHO1)		*Dedalo*
(CL)	02	*O'Higgins*
	D02	*Devonshire*
(LHA)	2	*Saipan*
(LPD)	2	*Vancouver*
(LPH)	2	*Iwo Jima*
(MCS)	2	*Ozark*
(AGF)	3	*La Salle*
	C3	*La Argentina*
(CL)	03	*Prat*
(LHA)	3	*Da Nang*
(LPH)	3	*Okinawa*
(C4)		*General Belgrano*
(CL)	04	*Latorre*
(CG)	4	*Little Rock*
(LHA)	4	*Belleau Wood*
(LPD)	4	*Austin*
(C5)		*9 de Julio*
(CG)	5	*Oklahoma City*
(LHA)	5	*Nassau*
(LPD)	5	*Ogden*
(CLG)	6	*Providence*
	D06	*Hampshire*
(LPD)	6	*Duluth*
(CLG)	7	*Springfield*
(LCC)	7	*Mount McKinley*
(LPD)	7	*Cleveland*
(LPH)	7	*Guadalcanal*
(LPD)	8	*Dubuque*
	R08	*Bulwark*
	R09	*Ark Royal*
(CGN)	9	*Long Beach*
(LPD)	9	*Denver*
(LPH)	9	*Guam*
(CG)	10	*Albany*
	L10	*Fearless*
(LPD)	10	*Juneau*
(LPH)	10	*Tripoli*
	A11	*Minas Gerais*
(CG)	11	*Chicago*
(CVS)	11	*Intrepid*
	L11	*Intrepid*
(LPD)	11	*Coronado*
(LPH)	11	*New Orleans*
	R11	*Vikrant*

	C12	*Tamandare*
(CG)	12	*Columbus*
(CVS)	12	*Hornet*
	D12	*Kent*
(LCC)	12	*Estes*
(LPD)	12	*Shreveport*
(LPH)	12	*Inchon*
	R12	*Hermes*
(LPD)	13	*Nashville*
(LSD)	13	*Casa Grande*
(LPD)	14	*Trenton*
(LSD)	14	*Rushmore*
(LPD)	15	*Ponce*
(LSD)	15	*Shadwell*
(CVT)	16	*Lexington*
	D16	*London*
(CG)	16	*Leahy*
(LCC)	16	*Pocono*
(LSD)	16	*Cabildo*
(CG)	17	*Harry E. Yarnell*
(LCC)	17	*Taconic*
(LSD)	17	*Catamount*
	D18	*Antrim*
(CG)	18	*Worden*
(LSD)	18	*Colonial*
(CVA)	19	*Hancock*
	D19	*Glamorgan*
(CG)	19	*Dale*
(LCC)	19	*Blue Ridge*
(LSD)	19	*Comstock*
	C20	*Tiger*
(CVS)	20	*Bennington*
	D20	*Fife*
(CG)	20	*Richmond K. Turner*
(LCC)	20	*Mount Whitney*
(LSD)	20	*Donner*
	21	*Melbourne*
	C21	*Canarias*
	D21	*Norfolk*
(CG)	21	*Gridley*
(CG)	22	*England*
(LSD)	22	*Fort Marion*
	D23	*Bristol*
(CG)	23	*Halsey*
(CG)	24	*Reeves*
(CGN)	25	*Bainbridge*
(CG)	26	*Belknap*
(LSD)	26	*Tortuga*
(CG)	27	*Josephus Daniels*

(LSD)	27	Whetstone
(CG)	28	Wainwright
(LSD)	28	Thomaston
(CG)	29	Jouett
(LSD)	29	Plymouth Rock
(CG)	30	Horne
(LSD)	30	Fort Snelling
(CVA)	31	Bon Homme Richard
(CG)	31	Sterett
(LSD)	31	Point Defiance
	TA31	Galicia
(CG)	32	William H. Standley
(LSD)	32	Spiegel Grove
(CG)	33	Fox
(LSD)	33	Alamo
(CVA)	34	Oriskany
(CG)	34	Biddle
(LSD)	34	Hermitage
(CGN)	35	Truxtun
(LSD)	35	Monticello
(CGN)	36	California
(LSD)	36	Anchorage
(CGN)	37	South Carolina
(DDG)	37	Farragut
(LSD)	37	Portland
(CGN)	38	Virginia
(CVS)	38	Shangri-La
(DDG)	38	Luce
(LSD)	38	Pensacola
(CGN)	39	Texas
(DDG)	39	Macdonough
(LSD)	39	Mount Vernon
(CGN)	40	Mississippi
(LSD)	40	Fort Fisher
(DDG)	40	Coontz
(CGN)	41	Arkansas
(CVA)	41	Midway
(DDG)	41	King
(CVA)	42	Franklin D. Roosevelt
(DDG)	42	Mahan
(CVA)	43	Coral Sea
(DDG)	43	Dahlgren
(DDG)	44	William V. Pratt
(DDG)	45	Dewey
(DDG)	46	Preble
	A59	Deutschland
(CVA)	59	Forrestal

	C60	Mysore
(CV)	60	Saratoga
(BB)	61	Iowa
(CVA)	61	Ranger
(BB)	62	New Jersey
(CV)	62	Independence
(BB)	63	Missouri
(CV)	63	Kitty Hawk
(BB)	64	Wisconsin
(CVA)	64	Constellation
(CVAN)	65	Enterprise
(CVA)	66	America
(CVA)	67	John F. Kennedy
(CVAN)	68	Chester W. Nimitz
(CVAN)	69	Dwight D. Eisenhower
(CA)	70	Canberra
(CVN)	70	Carl M. Vinson
(CA)	73	St. Paul
	C74	Delhi
	81	Almirante Grau
	82	Coronel Bolognesi
	83	Capitan Quinones
	84	Babur
	R97	Jeanne d'Arc
	R98	Clemenceau
	C99	Blake
	R99	Foch
(CA)	134	Des Moines
(CA)	139	Salem
(CA)	148	Newport News
	L153	Nafkratoussa
	C550	Vittorio Veneto
	C554	Caio Duilio
	D602	Suffren
	D603	Duquesne
	D610	Tourville
	C611	Colbert
	D612	de Grasse
	C802	de Zeven Provincien
(DD)	963	Spruance
(DD)	964	Paul F. Foster
(DD)	965	Kincaid
(DD)	966	Hewitt

(DD)	967	*Elliott*
(DD)	968	*Arthur W. Radford*
(DD)	969	*Peterson*
(DD)	970	*Caron*
(DD)	971	*David R. Ray*
(DD)	972	*Oldendorf*
(DD)	973	*John Young*
(DD)	974	*Comte de Grasse*
	L9021	*Ouragan*
	L9022	*Orage*

Photo Credits

Argentinian Official   9, 10, 11
Chilean Official   2, 15, 16, 17
Dutch Official   36
French Official   18, 21, 22, 23, 25, 26
Greek Official   28
Ambrose Greenway   39
Indian Official   29, 30, 31
Italian Navy   33, 34
Litton Industries   79
Marineamt   27
MoD   45, 46, 48, 49, 50, 53, 54, 111, 117, 123
Novosti Press Agency   107, 110, 116, 119, 121
Pakistan Official   38
Royal Australian Navy   12
Skyfotos   115
Spanish Official   41, 43
US Navy   4, 57, 59, 60, 62, 63, 64, 66, 67, 70, 71, 73, 74, 75, 77, 83, 84, 85, 87, 89, 90, 92, 93, 97, 98, 100, 101, 103, 104
Wright & Logan   14, 40, 106

Line Drawings
Bernard Ireland   19, 37, 52, 55, 69, 81, 108

Index

Ogden (*USA*)   86
O'Higgins (*Chile*)   16
Okinawa (*USA*)   82
Oklahoma City (*USA*)   67
Oktiabrskaia Revoliutsiia (*USSR*)   122
Oldendorf (*USA*)   78
Orage (*France*)   25
Oriskany (*USA*)   62
Otlikhnyi (*USSR*)   110
Otvazhnyi (*USSR*)   110
Ouragan (*France*)   25
Ozark (*USA*)   106

Paul F. Foster (*USA*)   78
Pensacola (*USA*)   89
Peterson (*USA*)   78
Plymouth Rock (*USA*)   91
Pocono (*USA*)   96
Point Defiance (*USA*)   91
Poncé (*USA*)   86
Portland (*USA*)   89
Prat (*Chile*)   16
Preble (*USA*)   76
Provedennyi (*USSR*)   110
Providence (*USA*)   67
Provornyi (*USSR*)   110

Raleigh (*USA*)   88
Ranger (*USA*)   59
Reeves (*USA*)   74
Richmond K. Turner (*USA*)   74
Roosevelt (see Franklin D. Roosevelt) (*USA*)   61
Rushmore (*USA*)   92

St. Paul (*USA*)   105
Saipan (*USA*)   80
Salem (*USA*)   102
Saratoga (*USA*)   59
Sdergiannyi (*USSR*)   110
Sea Control Ship (*USA*)   84
Sevastopol (*USSR*)   112
Shadwell (*USA*)   92
Shangri-La (*USA*)   62
Shreveport (*USA*)   86
Silnyi (*USSR*)   116
Slava (*USSR*)   118
Slavnyi (*USSR*)   110
Smelyi (*USSR*)   110

Smetlinyi (*USSR*)   110
Soobrazitelvyi (*USSR*)   110
South Carolina (*USA*)   69
Spiegel Grove (*USA*)   91
Sposobnyi (*USSR*)   110
Springfield (*USA*)   67
Spruance (*USA*)   78
Steregushchyi (*USSR*)   110
Sterrett (*USA*)   75
Strognyi (*USSR*)   110
Storozheroy (*USSR*)   116
Stroynyi (*USSR*)   110
Suffren (*France*)   23
Sverdlov (*USSR*)   122
Svirepyi (*USSR*)   116

Taconic (*USA*)   96
Tamandaré (*Brazil*)   14
Tarawa (*USA*)   80
Texas (*USA*)   68
Thomaston (*USA*)   91
Tiger (*UK*)   50
Tortuga (*USA*)   92
Tourville (*France*)   24
Trenton (*USA*)   86
Tripoli (*USA*)   82
Tromp (*Netherlands*)   36
Truxtun (*USA*)   71

Vancouver (*USA*)   88
Varyag (*USSR*)   109
Vikrant (*India*)   29
25 de Mayo (*Argentina*)   9
Vinson (see Carl M. Vinson)   55
Virginia (*USA*)   68
Vittorio Veneto (*Italy*)   32
Vladivostok (*USSR*)   112

Wainwright (*USA*)   75
Whetstone (*USA*)   92
William H. Standly (*USA*)   75
William V. Pratt (*USA*)   76
Wisconsin (*USA*)   99
Worden (*USA*)   74

Zhdanov (*USSR*)   122
Zheleznyakov (*USSR*)   120